BETTER OFF WORKING WILD

How changing the way we work can make us all better off

By Jeannette Pearce and Sara Turnbull

Orders: Please contact orders@betteroffedits.com

ISBN: 978-1-8381266-0-5

First published March 2020

WORKING WILD IS A WAY OF WORKING THAT MAKES US ALL BETTER OFF. IT'S AN APPROACH THAT LETS YOU AND YOUR TEAM – BE THEY COLLEAGUES, EMPLOYEES OR EMPLOYERS – BE MORE HUMAN, ENGAGE DEEPLY WITH OTHERS AND RECONNECT TO THE NATURAL WORLD THROUGH WORK. IT BRINGS YOU JOY AND DOESN'T EXHAUST YOU, OTHERS OR THE ENVIRONMENT, WHILE ENABLING COLLECTIVE SUCCESS THAT RESPECTS ENVIRONMENTAL LIMITS AND HUMAN NEEDS IN WAYS THAT CURRENT WAYS OF WORKING AND TRADITIONALLY NARROW DEFINITIONS OF SUCCESS DO NOT.

PREFACE

Throughout our work as entrepreneurs, employees, volunteers and now authors, our desire to enjoy our work while doing something good has evolved into wanting everyone's working lives to evolve and improve. Put simply, we want work to be better.

When we say we 'want work to be better', we are talking from hard experience. We've slept under our desks and very nearly been crushed by the volume of work and our approach to it. At those times we longed for and were refuelled by trips to wild mountains and beaches. Driving wind, heavy rain and cold water healed our pain.

We know it isn't just us. We've both seen colleagues, friends and family give themselves up in the name of 'a career', 'success' and 'progress'. By knowing first-hand how easily things can go wrong, we've been able to draw on our hard-won experience to build the strategies we call **Working Wild**. We hope to help you restructure the way you operate to enable you to work better.

Over time we have developed, tested and refined a set of practical tools for Working Wild. These will support you to change not just the way you work but the way your team works. You'll want to use them your way, grabbing those that seem right for the job in hand and discarding any that don't seem relevant to you. We preface our toolkit with a discussion of what's broken about the current work model and we set out some principles and attitudes for Working Wild by working better. But we won't sulk if you ignore the theory and dive straight into the practice. This is as much your book as it is ours and we want you to find your own wild way through it.

Please think of this book as the call of the wild: a call to the deepest part of you, inviting you to connect with the wild within you and the wild beyond you. This is not only a call to you as a manager, employer, employee, team member or client, but as a parent, child or friend. It asks you to remember and make space for your humanity and the wild in your work life, to reconnect with the humanity inside you and the nature that is you.

This is a simple, liveable philosophy and practice born of what we have learned (often the hard way) about living and working in a gentler, kinder way. We share it in the hope that it will help you to change the way you work and become genuinely better off as a result. Who knows, it may even help create a shift in society and economy that helps us all be better off, too?

Contents

Contents

01

WORK IS NOT WORKING

Work. Huh. Yeah.

What is it good for?

Absolutely nothing.

Let's say it again. We said:

Work. Huh. Yeah.

What is it good for?

Definitely not absolutely nothing.

Listen y'all[1]

Work puts food on the table.

Work puts a roof over your head.

Work can change the world.

Work can also change you.

Yet for too many people, work just isn't working: they feel underpaid, overworked, exploited, undervalued, bored, fractious or all of the above. So often work can leave us feeling disconnected from ourselves, each other and our environment.

We believe work is broken and offer **Working Wild** as an antidote. Working Wild is for everyone who has finished a day exhausted, frustrated and feeling poorer for it. It's for anyone with an inkling that working life doesn't have to be this way. And for anyone who doesn't want work to estrange us from our better selves, from others and from nature.

---

[1] To be sung to the tune of Edwin Starr's Motown hit *War* (1970).

Who are we?

We are work activists and wild advocates: we are also business leaders who have done many types of job and worked with many kinds of teams and organisations. Many would label us entrepreneurs – social and even serial entrepreneurs. But mostly we are just workers who love doing what we do. And what we love to do is run great organisations spurred by social missions and packed with empowered people. We are deeply passionate about the social and economic change that comes when you get small businesses and charities working in their communities.

We, Sara and JP, first met in 2014 across a boardroom table at City Hall in London. Not knowing one another, we were each surprised to hear the other introduce themselves at the table in the same way: 'I help businesses be more social and charities be more enterprising.'

At the time, along with other work roles, we were both running workspaces for small creative and social businesses in London, growing between us some 180,000 square feet of affordable creative workspace and supporting around 300 small businesses. On that particular day, we were at City Hall to advise the Mayor of London (at that time Boris Johnson) on policy and funding to help keep our city a creative and affordable place in which to work.

Knowing each other as we do today, we each recognise in the other someone who's been driven by work or, rather, driven to work and be self-sufficient from an early age.

We both spent a lot of time outdoors when growing up and know for sure that this has shaped us and continues to nourish our souls. When we first entered the world of work as teenagers, 50 miles and 10 years apart, we each had a clear vision that we didn't want to become someone who wore a suit to work, hated their stressful job and needed holidays to relax. As young idealists, we wanted to enjoy every day and believed fundamentally that we could enjoy work and use it to do good. Not much has changed.

Over our combined 55 years of work, we've run bars, markets, charities and creative businesses and been cleaners, waitresses (sadly not in a cocktail bar) and chief executives. We've rigged lights, designed scenery and made lots of stuff with our hands. We've provoked, supported and collaborated across the public, private and third sectors, creating strategies and impact through our work for government, housing associations, global brands, railways, mayors, fintech masterminds, rock bands, cultural icons, landowners, forests and farmers. We've managed venues, run global marketing accounts, established and grown social enterprises, led sustainability strategies for cities, and run social and creative workspaces.

Between us we've mentored and supported around 1,200 entrepreneurs, businesses, charities and social enterprises through all stages of development. Our enterprise training, cultural events and community engagement programmes have reached more than 50,000 people and made a significant social impact. Overall, we have led and managed organisations that have generated in excess of £10m turnover.

Most importantly, by moving through lots of industries and roles, we have carved careers for ourselves that allow us to address the social and environmental issues we are passionate about. We have shaped roles and created wealth in the broadest sense for ourselves, others, the communities we share and the environment in which we all live.

Doing all of this hasn't always been easy and we haven't always been easy on ourselves (or others) when doing it. We have felt knackered, thrilled, passionate, challenged and, at times, it seemed we were running solely on adrenaline as we came close to workaholism and burnout. Seeing ourselves and others do this, we've learned that how you work is as important as why and where you work.

Who are you?

Now your turn, gentle reader: how has work been working out for you so far? Are you an employee, colleague, employer or do you work alone? Why do you work and how do you do your best work? What do you love about your working life and which parts aren't working for you?

Although your answers to these questions are, of course, deeply personal, we can guarantee you will recognise yourself in at least one entry (if not more) on the list of common work disorders we've put together on the following pages. We ask you now to rate yourself in relation to how you approach your work, and how it makes you feel. By filling this out, we can really start to get to the bottom of what's brought you here, to this book and to us.

How is work working for you? Self-diagnostic check	
Are you...	**Details**
Addicted to work?	Overworking – riding the high of feeling important, strong and in control at work.
Bored of work?	Bored by the content of the role, the monotonous daily rhythm or the lack of joy.
Burned by purpose?	Driven mad, lonely or close to breaking point by pursuit of purpose at the cost of self.
Caught in the parent trap?	Not being able to afford the time to parent how you want or childcare costs more than you can earn.
Constantly on?	On your device at all hours – constantly on but distracted and not tuned in and focused.
Dislocated?	Long and/or stressful commute, long-distance travel or isolated at home.
Emotionally drained?	Lost in gossip, politics, an abusive or otherwise emotionally exhausting culture.
Financially insecure?	The feast or famine of being freelance, the zero-hour contract or the gig economy.
In work poverty?	Working an extra job (or jobs) to make up for the low pay of the first.
Irrational and irritable?	Struggling to manage your responses – when it's wrong the whole world knows it!

How is work working for you? Self-diagnostic check			
Never	Sometimes	Often	Why? When? How?

How is work working for you? Self-diagnostic check	
Are you...	**Details**
Managed by eejits?	Work would be brilliant if only the boss would let you get on or unblock the path.
Masking the self?	Muting or exaggerating yourself to create a professional image or fit in.
Micromanaged or micromanaging?	Can't trust or be trusted with the details so you get in the way of your colleagues.
Poor in purpose?	Income is high but meaning is low – you feel empty or unfulfilled.
Pulling the weight of others?	Feeling like you are putting in more than other people who don't seem to be accountable.
Trapped by responsibility?	You don't want to let your people/organisation down and so can't leave until after the next…
Taking it (out at) home?	Work takes so much out of you that when you get home you take it out on yourself and others.
Time starved?	Always pushing through, regularly doing longer hours from which you can't recover.
Wanting more?	Plodding along – not having a bad time but needing a bigger challenge and perhaps a new field?

How is work working for you? Self-diagnostic check			
Never	Sometimes	Often	Why? When? How?

How did you do? Of course, it is easy to suffer from one or more of these symptoms and to blame yourself or your colleagues for what's going wrong. Perhaps you think you just need to suck it up – after all, that's why they call it 'work'. Alternatively, you may think you need a change and feel hopeful that there is a way out by changing sector, job or even the format of employment, for example, by working part-time or for yourself.

But what if neither you nor your company is broken? What if work itself isn't working?

And, more importantly, how did it come to be this way?

What is work?

Work in and of itself can bring great delight and pleasure. We all need to work – not just to meet our economic needs or to look after ourselves, but to contribute to and engage with society.

Naturally, we don't just mean paid work. There are plenty of things most of us aren't paid to do that still really need to be done, whether that's food shopping, housework, raising children, caring for parents or the sick or doing voluntary work. Unfortunately, little of this is recognised as work because there's no financial value assigned to it. It's what we do when we're not making money. It's what we're driven or expected to do and, although everyone kicks off when it's not done, we're expected to do it quietly, without payment and without any reward beyond the sense of a job well done.

In the 19th and 20th centuries, most people's places of work moved from kitchens, houses, workshops, barns, fields and communities to factories and then offices, distribution centres and call centres. Simultaneously, work changed from being mostly self-determined – historically, many skilled workers worked for themselves and came together with local traders with similar skills through guilds – to something carried out from a position five layers deep in a management hierarchy.

So complete a transformation has this been that today 84 per cent of UK workers are employees, with more than 70 per cent of businesses defined as corporate.[2]

Just four per cent of employers are not-for-profit or part of the government.[3] Yes, there is an increase in alternatives – slashies[4] and freelancers, social enterprises and purpose-driven organisations, co-working and community-focused workspaces. These enable sole traders and micro businesses to work with and alongside one another and help to address the pressing need to be in good company for those who often work alone. But, overall, most people in paid work in the UK now work for organisations compelled by their legal structures to make and distribute profit to external shareholders,[5] while only a minority of people work actively to distribute rather than accumulate wealth.

The effects of this have been catastrophic. With most jobs and most work now operating according to an entirely industrial formula, we have seen wealth

---

[2] Office for National Statistics (2019).

[3] Office for National Statistics (2019).

[4] People engaged in more than one career, for example a lawyer/film producer.

[5] 'The first organisation structured to make profit was the East India Company in 1600. Before then, companies existed but only for social purposes (libraries, universities, etc). The rise of the use of incorporated companies to accumulate wealth goes hand in hand with colonisation.' *New Internationalist* (2002).

gaps expand and biodiversity shrink while corporations, whose wealth exceeds that of many nations, carry out ecocide[6] in the name of business as usual.

'We, the people, have lost control. Corporations, these legal fictions that we ourselves created two centuries ago, now have more rights, freedoms and powers than we do.' Kalle Lasn[7]

It's quite simple. By being complicit in an economic system founded on growth and success at any cost – a system that externalises the true costs to companies of their impact on people and the environment – we are exhausting our natural as well as social capital. Just imagine: business and industry are responsible for more than 18 per cent of the UK's carbon emissions[8] and 32 million tonnes of waste[9] on an annual basis.

The result? A dehumanising system that reduces many of us to cogs in the machine, disconnected from who we really are in the midst of a toxic and exhausted environment. A system in which nature, just like us, has been reduced to a resource to be used.

This leads us not just to climate change, the single biggest threat to all life on our planet, but also to the following significant crises.

---

[6] Ecocide is the decline or destruction of ecosystems by human activity or other causes. It emerged as a concept in the 1970s. In 2010, lawyer and campaigner Polly Higgins submitted a proposal to the United Nations, calling for ecocide to be included as an international crime by the International Criminal Court.

[7] Lasn, Kalle (2001) *Culture Jam: How to Reverse America's Suicidal Consumer Binge – and Why We Must,* HarperCollins.

[8] Department for Business, Energy and Industrial Strategy (2020).

[9] Department for Environment, Food and Rural Affairs (2019).

The five significant crises		
	Crisis	**Overview**
1	**Climate change**	**Can we survive extinction?** The need for a stable climate and resilience at the personal, local, national and international level in the face of rising sea levels, droughts, floods, climate migration, etc.
2	**Speed of change**	**Can we beat the robots or will we join them?** Technology is accelerating beyond anything experienced before. As artificial intelligence, biotech and IT develop, how can we keep up with the changes and retain our humanity?
3	**Biodiversity and food security**	**How and what will we eat?** The significant and unprecedented loss of biodiversity[10] has profound impacts for the food chain. The loss of pollinators for food crops is of particular concern and threatens human food security with significant health impacts.
4	**Disconnection**	**Will we ever feel whole and part of something again?** The extreme isolation and insulation from one's true self and others caused by distance, distraction, geography and technology. Increasing isolation from our place in the natural world.
5	**Common story[11]**	**What is our future and is there a place in it for me?** The lack of a clear vision for society on a national or international level that addresses the crises above and the myriad other issues facing humanity in a common, positive story.

[10] WWF's *Living Planet Report* provides a good introduction to this if you'd like to understand the scale and range of the loss of plants and animals.

[11] To learn more about the loss of – and need for – a new common story, we recommend Rutger Bregman's *Utopia for Realists,* Yuval Noah Harari's *21 Lessons for the 21st Century* and *The Myth Gap* by Alex Evans."

Grim reading, isn't it?

All the more so because it needn't have been this way. Things could and should have changed some 50 years ago when women entered the job market *en masse*, transforming the heteronormative culture in which the man worked outside the home to earn money while the woman worked inside the house to raise a family in a happy home.

Here was an opportunity to change not just where we worked but the way in which we worked (paid versus unpaid work, how work is valued), with positive implications not just for gender and equality but also for workers' rights.[12] The advent of automation, followed by the invention of labour-saving white goods, computers and now AI has so far proved to be another false dawn. While any or all of these should have reduced the amount of paid and unpaid work any of us has to do, it seems that most of us (especially women[13] and particularly those from BAME and/or working-class backgrounds[14]) are now working more, not less.

In short, despite changes in corporate law, urbanisation, family structure and technology, jobs in general are still constrained by expectations as rigid as those enforced on the employees of Victorian factories.

Things could and should have changed, but they didn't.

But we can change them now. We can do it by **Working Wild**.

---

[12] Surely if human beings were economically rational, when women entered the workforce some men would have started to leave the workforce and shift to working inside the home. Instead, while women's employment rate has increased, men's has remained steady (and it's not like there is any less housework or child rearing to do). So, on balance, more people are doing more work (paid and unpaid).

[13] Petriglieri, Jennifer (2019) *Couples That Work,* Penguin Life.

[14] Germano, Maggie (2019) 'Women are working more than ever, but they still take on most household responsibilities', *Forbes,* 27 March.

What is Working Wild?

We need a radical rethink of our entire relationship with work and the wild.

Let's start with 'wild' – a word that means many things to many people. For many it conjures up the remote, the uninhabited, the uncultivated powers of the natural world. It's adventure and the great outdoors: wide open spaces, devastating beauty and desolate expanses of land.

But for us, wild is so much more than that.

Wild is a natural state: not tamed or domesticated.

To be wild can also be to lack reason… like taking the 'wildest of guesses'.

It can drench us in fantasy through our wildest and most unimaginable dreams.

Wild permits us to grow unkempt and unchecked like a rambling plant or when we run wild with reckless abandon. We can be wild about music, food, hobbies or sport and less than wild about Brussels sprouts or our friend's new lover.

We can be the alternative, the outsider, the unpredictably maverick wild card.

Wild can find us irrational, riotous, extravagant or rash and stir in us the strongest emotions, leaving us anger fuelled with wide, wide eyes and a temper flipped.

It can also shake off discipline and restraint, indulging us in the wildest of parties.

For us, then, when we say wild, we essentially mean free, honest, interconnected and at our most creative. Nature thrives when it is left wild to find its own way and we, like everything in nature, thrive when we have space to grow and are part of a greater whole.

Wild is when we are not bogged down by belongings but focus instead on belonging. Belonging to that greater whole of nature.

Sadly so much of modern work is the antithesis of wild.

Work traditionally fences us in and we've been complicit in allowing it to – searching for ourselves in our achievements, to-do lists and promotions. We now battle to know ourselves in our life and work, lost in a constant stream of emails, messages and status updates that create new digital fences.

But the wild resists fences – connecting to your wildness will help you find joy by climbing over or levelling fences in your (work) life.

Which is why we are advocating not just for the wild but Working Wild – a total and radical rethink of the system of work that addresses its broken elements.

Of course, if being truly wild is to be truly free, then a huge part of Working Wild is to rewild the self by allowing you to be as natural and true to yourself as possible in your work role. In *Feral,* George Monbiot describes how he found in himself 'an unmet need for a wilder life … scratching at the walls of this life, hoping to find a way into a wider space beyond.'[15] We need to bring that sense of a wider space into our closed, fenced-in workplaces. We must enable our souls to speak and create with honesty and authenticity in our working as well as our personal lives. We must drop the roles we play at work and bring all the rainbow shades of our true selves to work with us. And we need to remember to give ourselves – and those we love and work with – the permission to be who they are, wherever they are, while reminding ourselves above all that 'No one is more youer than you.'[16]

Whether your work role requires you to wear a uniform or pearls, work shifts or rule the roost, you are quite probably thinking: 'How possible is this?' But the true question is: 'What is the cost of not trying?'

---

[15] Monbiot, George (2013) *Feral: Rewilding the Land, Sea and Human Life,* Penguin.

[16] Dr Seuss (1959) *Happy Birthday to You,* HarperCollins Children's Books.

Quite simply, we need to be alone and with ourselves. We need to connect deeply with all aspects of ourselves. Whether we do this first at home, in the prayer room or on a long mountain trek, rewilding the self is about reconnecting to the wild in you.

For many of us, that may mean using nature and time outdoors to refresh ourselves with a change of scenery. Most of us need to get outdoors in the elements – and in our element – to truly feel ourselves. (For us it's water, mountains and forests.) It is here that things are stripped back to the essentials so we can hear our true selves; not our panicked, stressed or striving selves. It is here that we can meet the wild within. We can connect again to our true selves by reconnecting to the natural world and our place in it. We can reconnect to awe and see ourselves as stewards and creatures in a complex and extraordinary world.

Ultimately, by going not just into nature but into the self and into the wild and messy bits of both, we can pay attention to our intuition: a huge stockpile of data and observations we can access rapidly to make sound judgments about the best thing to do.[17] That's when we can stand strong and reconnect with each other.

As educator Kurt Hahn put it: 'There is more in you than you know.'[18] Recognising this is what lets you take the next step, confident in your ability to choose the company you keep. Being in good company is a no-brainer: who wouldn't want to be among the best of friends, in a happy family or a cooperative and collaborative workplace? But how many of us really are?

---

[17] Hine, Megan (2017) *Mind of a Survivor: What the Wild has Taught Me About Survival and Success*, Hodder & Stoughton.

[18] The full quote commonly attributed to Kurt Hahn is 'There is more in us than we know if we could be made to see it; perhaps, for the rest of our lives we will be unwilling to settle for less.'

Fundamentally, as an employee you are often only able to decide the quality and character of the company you choose to work for and the company of your co-workers. Those of you who own, lead, manage or hold shares in any organisation can do even more. You can influence and create good companies by improving the quality and character of the team and the work culture, the products and services, the quality of the pay and conditions and the leadership and management style. You might do it by aligning the purpose and impact of your organisation with issues and groups you care about, or by supporting individuals to create, self-manage, develop and grow.

You know you are in good company when you are allowed to be human. Any company that links you to your environment and the people around you or the causes you care about will ultimately give you the cosy feeling of being in good company while nurturing the wildest version of you.

We've been Working Wild ourselves, in our businesses and with our clients. And now we'd like to take it on with you. To help you with this aspect of your life. For your life's work, your team and family. Because, make no mistake, making work work for everyone will make us all better off. The way most of us work is not only breaking us but our families and friendship networks, the economy and the environment. Changing the way we work and our attitude to work has the potential not only to help us on an individual and personal level but also to help address the five major crises we've identified – one step at a time.

02

FIX WORK BY WORKING WILD

A confession before we start. We're not wholly there yet. When trying to work wild we haven't always got it right. More than once, we've taken a big step in the right direction only to find we have actually made our lives harder.

Our mistakes have taught us that Working Wild isn't just about going into the wild and doing our work. Writing a business plan in a boat, which might as well have been a moving bathtub, didn't work out so well for JP. Sara fared no better when she tried to run a business and hold down a proper job while living off grid on a toiletless narrowboat (without any renovation funds). And our attempts to deliver meaningful client work from the back of a motorbike or on a ferry (with no wifi or laptop) also didn't prove too successful.

Don't get us wrong: Working Wild certainly does involve getting in the wild. In fact, since we started experimenting with Working Wild we have enjoyed many brilliant conference calls at the beach, client meetings around the fire and have successfully expanded our work environment and timetable to allow more freedom. But while all these things have brought us real joy and immense creativity, there is much to be said for working in a quiet room, at a real desk and alongside a great team. So we've discovered that Working Wild is as much about how we work and the attitude we bring to work as it is about becoming a working nomad. It's about being our true selves at work.

This is why we've defined the following attitudes and tools for Working Wild. We learned the hard way (so you don't have to) that making radical changes to an entire system is very difficult on your own. Instead, by arming you with the right attitudes and the right tools for the job – whatever job you have in mind – we can help you on your way. What happens after that will depend on where you've reached and how many of your colleagues, bosses, employees, shareholders and supporting friends and family you have brought with you on your journey.

Get attitude

Working Wild requires a shift in mindset and culture to a gentler, more human approach. The table on the following page sets out five attitudes needed to work wild, alongside the kind of bad attitudes that are likely to have caused many of the negative experiences that may have scarred you at work.

Broken Work attitudes		Working Wild attitudes
I am Consumer	→	**We are Nature**
The reduction of humanity to consumption. The loss of our link to each other and nature. Burying the self under stuff.		We are each a small part of the whole. That which harms the whole harms the individual and vice versa.
Sell Your Soul	→	**Create Joy**
Giving up oneself or the chance to know yourself in order to fit in or earn more.		Get absorbed in making beauty. Craft experiences that engage and move others. Dance your socks off.
More, More, More!	→	**Enough is Enough**
An obsession with growth as the only measure of success. Greed. No respect for limits to resources.		Understand and practise sufficiency. Enjoy abundance, wealth and comfort – just not at any cost.
When I Retire	→	**Own Your Breath**
Wishing your life away. Delaying hopes, dreams and even rest until they are earned by success.		Everything hangs on your next breath. You are the only constant in your life. Own your choices and habits.
Powercock	→	**Gentle Warrior**
The parading of power at the cost of others, fed by the ego and fear that weakness will be exposed.		Lead with love, bring people to a better place, fight fair and with principles.

Although these attitudes are arranged to help you clearly identify and define the two opposing ends of a spectrum, we freely acknowledge that few things in life are genuinely binary. The attitudes identified should, therefore, be considered a progression and a transition from one to the other, rather than as a case of one versus the other.

Let's look at these attitudes in more detail.

We are all suffering from the current economic system's best efforts to reduce us to consumers. As Tom Hodgkinson said 'In the current scheme of things, when we're not working, we're consuming. We suffer a strange split in our roles in society between that of worker and consumer, the oppressed and the courted.'[19]

This **I am Consumer** attitude is very limiting and perhaps even destructive to our souls. Such a way of thinking asks us to accept that humans are selfish creatures, set apart from each other and nature. Whereas, of course, **We are Nature** – not just part of nature but stewards with a responsibility and duty to nature (be that human nature or the natural world) that should underpin all the roles we play at work and the work we do. This includes the custodial development of people, ideas and innovation as well as carrying things through with ritual and care.

---

[19] Hodgkinson, Tom (2007) *How to be Free*, Penguin.

'WORK IS LOVE MADE VISIBLE.'[20]

[20] Gibran, Khalil (1923) *The Prophet*. BN Publishing.

When considering a child at play or a craftsperson at work, most people intrinsically 'get' this but how many of us bring love into the workplace? How have we accepted a dominant working culture where, for the most part, love and care are deemed 'soft skills' at best or, at worst, unwelcome and unprofessional weaknesses?

So let's turn that around, bring the love and **Create Joy** in our work life. We aren't saying that everyone needs to work in a creative or caring career. We mean that work, on most days, should be something you can bring joy to and create joy with. Even 'hard work' can be something in which we can find pure joy. Fail to do this and you run the risk of getting caught up in a **Sell Your Soul** attitude that finds us endlessly rebranding ourselves and selling ourselves short.

When **I am Consumer** and **Sell Your Soul** thinking combine, you're on a fast track to feeling trapped: earning more but rarely breaking even due to increasingly high expectations of what you need and deserve. Every pay rise or bonus you are lucky enough to receive will be spent twice over as your perceived needs expand to meet your new means. Here you'll be not just time poor but possibly poor in terms of the quality and quantity of your relationships.[21] This compulsion to work more despite increasing remuneration[22] is irrational and fuels the time-starved nature of work and life, minute by painful minute.

More, More, More!

---

[21] James, Oliver (2007) *The Selfish Capitalist: Origins of Affluenza,* Vermilion.

[22] To be precise, average working hours have fallen but 'while overall working hours have stalled, many lower paid workers are working less than they want to, while many of the rich are working more than they need to.' Skidelsky, Robert and Edward (2012) *How Much is Enough?: Money and the Good Life,* Penguin.

'Harder, better, faster, stronger.' Daft Punk[23]

'I wish I was a little bit taller, I wish I was a baller.' Skee-Lo[24]

Not knowing when to stop and digging so deep for so long that your adrenals pack in won't win you the admiring glances you may have earned in the 1980s. Fortunately, the doctrine of success predicated on sacrifice is becoming defunct. Still, how many of us really have a sense of when **Enough is Enough**? It's easy to work too hard for too long, depleting the self and then taking your work on holiday rather than really resting.[25] Is it because, deep within ourselves, we've yet to realise that we don't have to be more than enough? Or is it because our workloads have increased to the extent that we are now each expected to do more than the work of one person?[26] It's only when the body or mind breaks and we are forced to stop that we truly understand that no one is indispensable.

It all just keeps coming back to time.

What a terrible waste it would be to wait 20 years to be happy (**When I Retire**), when to **Own Your Breath** would have allowed you to live in and savour each moment – even the hard ones. Our breath is both our time and our energy in each moment. Our breath is where we are right now. Checking in on your breath is checking in on yourself. Are you holding your breath? Or are you making each breath count?

---

23 Bangalter, T, Birdsong, E and De Homem-Christo, G (2001) *Harder, Better, Faster, Stronger*, Paris, Virgin.

24 Harden, J and Roundtree, A (Skee-Lo) (1995) *I Wish*, Scotti Brothers Records.

25 Hesketh, Ian (2014) *Leaveism and Public Sector Reform: Will the Practice Continue?* Lancaster University Management School.

26 Schor, Juliet (1993) *The Overworked American: the Unexpected Decline of Leisure*, Basic Books.

Of course, it can be difficult to breathe at all, if there's a **Powercock** in the room.

'Even though worker capacity and motivation are destroyed when leaders choose power over productivity, it appears that bosses would rather be in control than have the organisation work well.'
Margaret J Wheatley[27]

Although everyone's got a bit of **Powercock** in them – selfish behaviour that comes from giving too much and being under pressure, lots of it, both real and perceived – you're in danger of becoming a first-class **Powercock** when you get the increasing sense that everything hangs on you and that, without you, the business will crumble. So in giving too much, you feel both angry at the opportunity cost and also justified in being upset and feeling let down by everyone. Ultimately, this leaves you conducting your work as though you're living in a state of war, armed with the misconception that it's perfectly all right to behave like an ass to anyone not feeding your war effort.

Naturally, this is going to be as bad for you as it is unbearable for everyone around you, so how can you be gentler while still being a warrior? Can you be charmingly disruptive, still taking on the fight but able to look after yourself and others with kindness? You can lead as a **Gentle Warrior** from any place in an organisation, not just from the top, by doing the battle of business with kindness, humility and compassion. This takes greater courage and strength than Powercocking, raging and pointing the way (your way = the only way) and requires guidance, nurturing and respect for others. To understand **Gentle**

[27] Wheatley, Margaret (2005) 'How is your leadership changing?' blogpost.

Warrior, think about the warrior in yoga – open poses with arms outstretched. These are poses of lightness and moderation, as well as strength.

Let's take some time now for a little reflection to explore your attitudes and behaviour in the context of what we've been talking about. Where on the scale from **Broken Work** attitude to **Working Wild** attitude do you sit? How do you think you are doing? Where do you think you could improve (if you're falling a bit short) and where is there cause for celebration (for the bits you're getting right)?

Grab yourself three different coloured pens.

- **With colour one** mark where you think you are on a scale of one to five (where one is a very Broken Work attitude and five is totally Working Wild). Do this thinking about where you are on a day-to-day basis.
- **With colour two** give yourself a score for how you behave and what your attitude is like when things get hard or you are really stressed.
- **With colour three** mark where you think you can get for each attitude within the next nine months.[28]

---

[28] In our work with our own teams and with clients, we often use nine months as a timescale for making significant changes on the basis that if a whole human being can be created in that time, surely we can change whatever it is that needs to be addressed. If you find that weird, by all means make a six-month or one-year plan.

Broken Work attitudes	1	2	3	4	5	Working Wild attitudes
I am Consumer The reduction of humanity to consumption. The loss of our link to each other and nature. Burying the self under stuff.						**We are Nature** We are each a small part of the whole. That which harms the whole harms the individual and vice versa.
Sell Your Soul Giving up oneself or the chance to know yourself in order to fit in or earn more.						**Create Joy** Get absorbed in making beauty. Craft experiences that engage and move others. Dance your socks off.
More, More, More! An obsession with growth as the only measure of success. Greed. No respect for limits to resources.						**Enough is Enough** Understand and practise sufficiency. Enjoy abundance, wealth and comfort – just not at any cost.
When I Retire Wishing your life away. Delaying hopes, dreams and even rest until they are earned by success.						**Own Your Breath** Everything hangs on your next breath. You are the only constant in your life. Own your choices and habits.
Powercock The parading of power at the cost of others, fed by the ego and fear that weakness will be exposed.						**Gentle Warrior** Lead with love, bring people to a better place, fight fair and with principles.

In starting your journey, ask what you can do to make the shift. What work do you need to do with others to break down the barriers to adopting these attitudes? Who can you ask for support and to hold you to account? Is this a journey you can share with friends and peers or as a team, or is it one you must walk alone?

Remember that attitudes are some of the hardest things you'll ever have to shift. Even when you think you've got it right by successfully changing the way you work, you might still make a poor choice or fall back into bad attitudes when the pressure is on. Certainly that's what we've found from our own experience. Don't worry if this sounds like you. Just dust yourself off and try again.

To start your shift, use the following tools to shake things up and help embed great choices and better ways of working. They will be there for you when you're moving forward. And, just as importantly, they will be there again should you need to restart – each time bringing you that bit closer to achieving your goal.

Choose your tools

Wouldn't it be great if we had the tools to create a working mindset that keeps us grounded, connects us to the real world and cultivates a sustainable and healthy attitude to work – thereby preventing us from hitting the wall, falling off the cliff or feeling disconnected? In what follows, we present an A-Z of tools to help you build a better way of working, one that balances your needs as an individual, a team member and part of the wider environment.

We've adopted, tried and tested these tools on ourselves, in our businesses and in the leadership teams and organisations we support through our work. While these tools work best when used preventatively rather than as a remedy, many will help you get out of a rut or navigate through a tricky period. Naturally, as with all tools, choosing the right one for the job is what's important. You can start at A and work your way through, or pick up the tool that best fits your need. The real magic happens when you start to apply several tools in combination.

Whoever you are, whatever your means and whatever you're working on now, these tools for Working Wild are for you. You might be working nights or long winter days, unable to see or feel the sun until the weekend and feeling as if you are stuck on a treadmill, not seeing enough of your loved ones. Maybe you are trying to keep on top of an endless to-do list or dressing as someone else and not bringing your true self to work. Whatever element of your work isn't working for you, look through the A-Z and find the tool you need right now to start changing your work (and life) for the better.

03

A-Z OF TOOLS FOR WORKING WILD

TO BE TRULY
ON, YOU NEED
TO SWITCH
OFF.

A

IS FOR AIRPLANE MODE

These days, the working week often starts on a Sunday (as people try to 'get ahead') and work often goes on into weekday evenings. But being constantly on call means you are never really fully anywhere. Insistent phone, text and email interruptions eat away at your time and focus. Being flexible and available may fill a need but it's no coincidence that the more 'on' we are, the more 'off' we seek to be – hence the recent increase in the popularity of mindfulness and yoga. Knowing when to switch off has benefits outside work, too, as being on all the time weakens relationships with partners, families and friends, and distracts you from your flow at work. If, as Jennifer Petriglieri says: 'undivided attention is the fuel of relationships,'[29] surely the best gift you can give yourself, your work and your loved ones is your full attention?

Your tech is there to serve you – not the other way around.
Resist the temptation to be continually on call.
Return to the analogue world and explore its delights.
Or stay in the digital one and get in the flow.
Do the virtual equivalent of closing your bedroom door when you were a teenager.
Claim your own space and own time to clear your mind.
Allow no interruptions.
Now we, or should we say you, have your full attention, who and what do you want to share it with?

---

[29] Petriglieri, Jennifer (2019) *Couples That Work*, Penguin Life.

'I OFTEN FEEL THAT I INHABIT TWO WORLDS: A MODERN, TECHNOLOGICAL ONE ... AND AN OLDER, SLOWER LIFE THAT IS A SENSUAL CONNECTION WITH EARTH, BODY, NATURAL ELEMENTS, FOOD AND PLACE – QUIETLY OLD-FASHIONED, EMBODIED EXISTENCE THAT STILL EXISTS AND NOURISHES, MOSTLY BECAUSE I CHOOSE TO MAKE IT SO.' LR HEARTSONG[30]

Ensuring the productivity of computer programmers at Microsoft was critical in the eighties and nineties. Although there were fewer digital calls on employees' attention in those days, colleagues popping by for chats created plenty of distraction. Coders were encouraged to wear hats to show they didn't want to be disturbed during their creative flow, the state in which sudden leaps and real magic occur. Programmer Brian Knapp said: 'This is very similar to playing music, writing, and painting. Imagine if Leonardo da Vinci was expected to paint the Mona Lisa in an open office space while his coworkers and manager would stop him mid stroke every 15 minutes to ask a question. Would he have ever painted it?'[31]

In the first few years of living on a houseboat with little access to electric power, Sara found airplane mode on her phone essential for saving her battery life between trips to the office. She continued to use the phrase (and function) **Airplane Mode** long after the electrics in her boat were up and running. What started as a survival technique had become a really useful way to give her time to think and reduce distractions. Sara quickly discovered that if people really need you while you are on **Airplane Mode**, they will come looking for you and shout to you from the riverbank.

---

[30] Heartsong, LR (2018) *To Kneel and Kiss the Earth: Inspiration from the Soul Artist Journal,* Hearthside Press.

[31] Knapp, Brian (2018) 'Why programmers wear headphones,' blogpost.

TWEAKS FOR YOU

→ Take control of your life by using **Airplane Mode** when you need to. Put your phone on **Airplane Mode** overnight, every night, and then extend into an hour a day, every day.

→ Choose when to stop and disconnect, allowing yourself to focus and find flow in what you are working on. Use the phrase 'I'm in **Airplane Mode**' to emphasise to yourself and others that you are choosing to focus.

SHIFTS FOR YOUR TEAM

→ Work with your team to agree tech etiquette and boundaries: how do you communicate and when? How soon is soon enough to expect a reply?

→ Consider a tech-free retreat for a big project with a deadline, whether for starting something new or managing a crisis.

JUMPS FOR YOUR ORGANISATION

→ Carve out time in the week and space in the workplace where **Airplane Mode** is the norm.

→ What's your organisational equivalent of the programmer's hat? How can you protect your team's ability to focus and find its creative flow? Could tools like Microsoft Teams and Slack help relieve your team of email- and phone-related interruption or will they become a new distraction?

TAKE YOUR
WORK
ON AN
ADVENTURE.

B

IS FOR BOLDLY GO

With technological innovation making it easier to work on the move or from multiple locations, it's possible to **Boldly Go** to work like never before. While some work still has to be done at a desk, there are now opportunities to be more flexible with how and where you work. If you have such freedom, that's great – but not everyone has work that can easily escape a physical workspace. Luckily, we don't mean that you literally have to go on an adventure every day with your work. It's how you bring an adventurous spirit and mindset to yourself and everything you do – work included – that matters.

Mountaineer John Amatt says: 'Adventure isn't hanging on a rope off the side of a mountain. Adventure is an attitude that we must apply to the day-to-day obstacles of life – facing new challenges, seizing new opportunities, testing our resources against the unknown and, in the process, discovering our own unique potential.'[32]

When you can, enjoy the benefits of not being desk-bound from nine to five.
Take your work on an adventure and bring adventure into your work.
How many explorers made great discoveries while wearing their power suit or pyjamas?
Equip yourself to go beyond what you already know.
Go where you don't feel comfortable.
Change the lens.

---

[32] Amatt, John (2019) *Outward Bound Lessons to Live a Life of Leadership*, Berrett-Koehler.

'LIFE IS EITHER A DARING ADVENTURE OR NOTHING. TO KEEP OUR FACES TOWARD CHANGE AND BEHAVE LIKE FREE SPIRITS IN THE PRESENCE OF FATE IS STRENGTH UNDEFEATABLE.' HELEN KELLER[33]

Step away from your desk and work on the wild side. Avoid the temptation to set up a lonely office for one at home, when you could be taking your work up a mountain, on a trek or a campervan tour. You can still be on an adventure even if you can only work remotely for an hour or half a day. Find new things and places. Cultivate the spirit to explore and a healthy attitude to risk doing things differently. Foster curiosity and different ways of thinking, find new perspectives and open up a freedom to roam in your mind, in the wild and at work. After all, how many breakthrough moments do any of us have at our desks

Kudos to ourselves for this one because, in writing this book, we have put this tool fully to the test. We've written it long-hand in notebooks, on blackboards, on receipts and even once on a bread bag. We've written it in parks, on sofas, on boats, on trains, at skate parks, in coffee shops, in howling gales, from our (sick) beds, on many floors and only very, very occasionally in an office. Physically together for just a fraction of the time, we worked on the project remotely online and over the phone. We soon started calling our remote collaborations *tech cwtch* – *'cwtch'* in Welsh (pronounced cutch) meaning a cuddle or a hug; a cubby hole or a cupboard (somewhere to store something safely). While we worked on this book our *tech cwtch* kept us feeling close, even though we were far away from one another. We were collaborating while at the same time boldly going on our separate adventures, running our respective companies, sail training, surfing, camping and generally spending more time with our loved ones.

---

[33] Keller, Helen (1940) *Let Us Have Faith,* Doubleday Doran.

TWEAKS FOR YOU

→ Where is it you'd most like to go? Can you take your work there and actually work better away from your desk? If you can then you are ready to **Boldly Go.**

→ Hone your kit to include only what you need to take your work anywhere (chargers, water bottle, packing cubes, notebooks, etc.). That way, if a meeting is cancelled or a train is delayed, you can turn it into an adventure and get your work done anywhere.

SHIFTS FOR YOUR TEAM

→ Have a plan for all the members of the team that allows them to **Boldly Go** somewhere once a year or as often as can be fitted in, based on their needs and those of the organisation.

→ Which members of the team have the most adventurous spirit? Can you get them to review your attitude to risk to help you benefit from being more bold?

JUMPS FOR YOUR ORGANISATION

→ Encourage everyone in your organisation to lead a 'full life' so in return you get creative and innovative employees who want to do well.

→ Focus on output not presenteeism by enabling radical mobile working, for example, a week of working half days by the beach or up a hill.

THE WAY WE DO THINGS ROUND HERE.

C

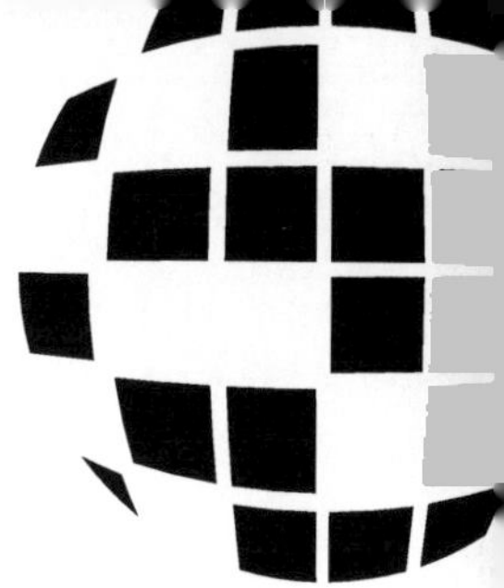

IS FOR CULTURE CLUB

Every place of work has its own culture, good or bad. Culture can't be forced but it can be cultivated – values, like grass, grow from the roots up. Deep down we all need to belong to a club with values that resonate and encourage our best work. A **Culture Club** approach is there to serve all its members, cherish your people and make them – and you – stronger. The aim is to avoid sticking-plaster approaches and top-down, surface-level perks that tie culture to results. Instead, foster an organisation that links individual needs with organisational requirements, born from a culture of care and understanding. Watch, listen and nurture as your culture evolves. Clubbing together makes work a process of co-creation that nurtures a rich and delicious culture.

Products and services can be copied: culture can't.
Culture isn't something you can fake or switch on and off.
You don't always see it or feel it, but you'll know when it's not right.
If what you say on the outside is different to what you do on the inside…
Trust us, people will know.

'THE MOST AMAZING THING ABOUT A CULTURE IS THAT ONCE IT'S STRONG, IT'S SELF-REPLICATING. EVEN THOUGH YOU'VE TAKEN A NUMBER OF CONSCIOUS ACTIONS TO IMPACT IT, YOU'LL KNOW YOU'VE SUCCEEDED WHEN IT IS TRULY NO LONGER ABOUT YOU.' KIM SCOTT[34]

Culture can be created even when you don't share a physical office, as demonstrated by Trello, an online platform for project management. They regularly celebrate what is unique about their own culture – their "no office" policy and the power of their platform to bring people together – with virtual away days. Each member of the Trello community is given a budget to run their own personal "awayday" based on their own passions. All the individual awaydays around the world take place simultaneously with staff sharing their experiences on their own Trello app.[35]

Culture Club was born in one of JP's companies in the late 90s as a way to collate and distil employees' thoughts on what the company wanted to do beyond its day-to-day work. Some ideas stuck and some fell by the wayside but all were given a fair hearing. That's why, 22 years later, the JPC team still keeps the faith with activities laid out in a **Culture Club** bible – a directory for getting the best out of the business. Lush, the 100% vegetarian cosmetics retailer, uses a similar approach in that, 'anyone can make a suggestion to any department. There are no lines in the sand … when the people working in the business can see that the business cares about them, they are more willing and able to go the extra mile to pull off the impossible. We want to make our mums proud.'[36]

---

[34] Scott, Kim (2017) *Radical Candor: How to Get What You Want by Saying What You Mean*, St Martin's Press.

[35] Trello website (2019).

[36] Lush website (2019).

TWEAKS FOR YOU

→ Be brave enough to propose social activities in and outside of work that will draw people closer together.

→ Write three to four lines describing the company you work for, imagining it not as a company but as a person. Consider this profile and how you feel about this character and how they behave. Is this someone you'd hang out with and respect? If not, what can you do about that?

SHIFTS FOR YOUR TEAM

→ Set-up a **Culture Club** where your team meet to look at what they need to make work work better for everyone. Be prepared to adopt and fund ideas and to advocate for them with leadership.

→ What do your team really need? If you are already paying them well how can you help them to be truly better off? Time and flexibility to parent well? Access to a (social enterprise) spa? Time for adventure?

JUMPS FOR YOUR ORGANISATION

→ Breed an innovation culture enabling your teams to bring you the initiatives, both social and structural, that can evolve and develop your business and team culture.

→ Put your people first. Prioritise staff in your business plan and constantly look for ways to create opportunities for growth – you will attract and retain great people that help you grow, too.

A STRONG NO CREATES ROOM FOR THE RIGHT YES.

D

IS FOR DO OR DO NOT

Every day we make small choices. You are either doing or you are not doing. You are either saying yes or no to something. Every single thing you have on your plate at any one time is something you've said yes to. It's all about choice – you fill your time with what you choose. You have said yes to reading this book (thank you) and no to looking at a website or watching TV. Saying yes and committing to seeing something through is fundamental to doing things well, but what about all the stuff you (didn't mean to) say yes to? How about those things that ended up on your plate because you didn't say no and this was taken as a de facto yes? And what about the opportunity cost – by agreeing to do something, you have effectively declined to do something else? Clearly, our choices shape the way we are. So permit yourself the luxury of the guilt-free choice to not do and not say yes to everything.

Today could be that amazing day – the one where life is how we want it to be.
We just have to choose for it to be or, rather, stop choosing for it NOT to be.
So decide – it's Do or Do Not.
Because deciding what not to do is as important as deciding what to do.
Say 'no' before the sheer weight of all those yeses breaks you.

'WITH A HAVING-IT-ALL SCRIPT RUNNING ON OVERDRIVE, YOU ARE ALMOST CERTAINLY DOING SOME THINGS BECAUSE YOU THINK YOU SHOULD DO THEM, RATHER THAN BECAUSE YOU REALLY NEED OR WANT TO.' JENNIFER PETRIGLIERI[37]

In *The Empire Strikes Back,* Yoda famously admonishes Luke Skywalker with the words: 'Do or do not. There is no try.' It's unlikely you got to this point in your life without oodles of lessons about focus, prioritising and 'just say no'. But how much of that stuck? Choosing to actively do the right thing (or the wrong thing) all adds up. Tim Ferris's podcast *How to Say No*[38] describes how once he started saying no, rather than losing out he actually started to succeed. The podcast includes great tips for saying no in such a way as to leave people feeling really good about you. Entrepreneur Jeff Olson[39] describes a phenomenon whereby small, repetitive and realistic incremental gains (the dos) generate a daily compound interest that builds into a cumulative gain of your actions, both positive and negative, over a long period of time. This can have a huge impact on your happiness by constantly building something up with your choices.

Edith Whitehead, one of Sara's early teammates, encouraged Sara to radically adopt the Pomodoro Technique – an anti-procrastination tool whereby you decide what to do and then set a timer for 25 minutes to get it done. Francesco Crillo started this in the late 1980s, using a tomato-shaped timer. Our company WorkWild now uses pomodoros (the tool, not the tomato) in our daily work practice as well as in sessions with clients. Our report *The Affordability Crisis* was structured and unlocked in a half day of pomodoros with a team of five organisations.

---

[37] Petriglieri, Jennifer (2019) *Couples That Work,* Penguin Life.

[38] Ferris, Tim (2017) *How to Say No,* podcast.

[39] Olson, Jeff (2013) *Slight Edge,* Gazelle.

TWEAKS FOR YOU

→ Gather together all your to-do lists into one place and do an audit of everything you've already said yes to. Which of these will you enjoy doing? Which ones have you no choice over? How many could you have said no to? On what are you choosing to spend your valuable time? Can you say a nice no to 25 per cent?

→ Think of a polite no as a complete sentence. Not 'No I can't because…' It's the dots that let in the yeses and leave us suddenly doing something we didn't want to do.

SHIFTS FOR YOUR TEAM

→ Replace long meetings with a work session that includes a set of pomodoros. If it's something worth doing, get on and do it: don't just talk about doing it later. That adds stress.

→ Question the need for habitual behaviour in the team: don't do things that you have always done just because you've always done them. Instead, make a positive choice to **Do or Do Not** for all your habitual workload, based on usefulness and necessity.

JUMPS FOR YOUR ORGANISATION

→ Make your organisation a safe place for people to say no. Make it clear that you are looking beyond 'yes-people' for those who remember that when they are saying yes to something, they are saying no to something else.

→ Invest time in training your people to be smart/clever 'no-sayers', who are able to recognise and say no effectively and so open up time for the yeses.

REST.
PART OF THE
PROCESS.
PART OF
THE JOY.

E IS FOR EASY NOW

Easy Now can be a greeting or a state of mind. It's as much about peace and quiet as it is about rest and pampering. Think about the sensation of relaxing in a hot, deep bath – it's surely no coincidence that Archimedes' eureka moment occurred in the tub. Meanwhile, in Chinese and Japanese culture, rest, respite and holidays are intrinsically linked to trees – so much so that the character for rest (休) depicts a person (人) beside a tree (木). And good things happen to people who spend time near trees. If you don't believe us, remember Isaac Newton and the apple and Siddhartha Gautama (the spiritual teacher who became known as the Buddha) finding enlightenment under a tree.

Time off leads to breakthroughs and better work outcomes.
Take time to reconnect and recharge.
Your 'easy' might be forest bathing.
Your easy might be recharging by volunteering.
Or special time spent with wonderful people in magical places.
Whatever your easy, it's time well spent that touches your soul and reignites your fire.

'THE HIGHEST PURPOSE IS TO HAVE NO PURPOSE AT ALL. THIS PUTS ONE IN ACCORDANCE WITH NATURE, IN HER MANNER OF OPERATION.' JOHN CAGE[40]

In his work on silence and creativity, John Lane notes: 'In an overstimulated and excessive world, silence is what connects us to the richness of the everyday moment of the wonder of being.'[41] It's why Quakers start their meetings in silence. There is power in just stopping, and stopping together. It's often only in silence that we realise what it is we need to talk about.

Sara first saw **Easy Now** in action when working on a project in Finland. The client group had a real sense of how to use silence and rest for the common good. At a critical moment in the project, the whole client group took six weeks' annual leave to celebrate midsummer. While the Finns left the city to enjoy the long days and fill up on saunas and nature, Sara and a team of Americans, Brits, Italians and Germans struggled with the idea that anything could be more important than the big deadline. Sara had been sleeping under her desk under a hi-vis jacket for some time, working around the clock to hit the same deadline. This episode taught her a lot about priorities and the value of silence. Many Finns don't tend to speak unless they have something to say but they will (unlike many Brits and most Japanese) tell you if they disagree with you. So meetings and projects reach an honest place where the participants stay quiet and wait for the right moment to speak.

---

[40] Cage, John (1961) *Silence: Lectures and Writings,* Wesleyan.

[41] Lane, John (2006) *The Spirit of Silence: Making Space for Creativity,* Green Books.

TWEAKS FOR YOU

→ Keep an open dialogue with your manager about your workload and energy levels and check in with your co-workers about theirs.

→ Remember the ratio of two ears and one mouth: take the time to listen carefully between the notes and resist the temptation to fill silence with noise.

SHIFTS FOR YOUR TEAM

→ Watch out for burnout and prevent it with time out. Insist people spread their holidays throughout the year and take a fortnight off at least once a year.

→ Start meetings with short silences or meditation sessions like those now being introduced by some schools into the first minutes of each class.

JUMPS FOR YOUR ORGANISATION

→ Set clear close-down dates in winter and summer (or whenever best suits your industry) to give your people a proper break.

→ Take a moment to imagine how the world would be if decisions over history had been taken by the calm, rested and quiet people rather than the loudest in the room. Reward people who hold their silence as well as those who love to speak up.

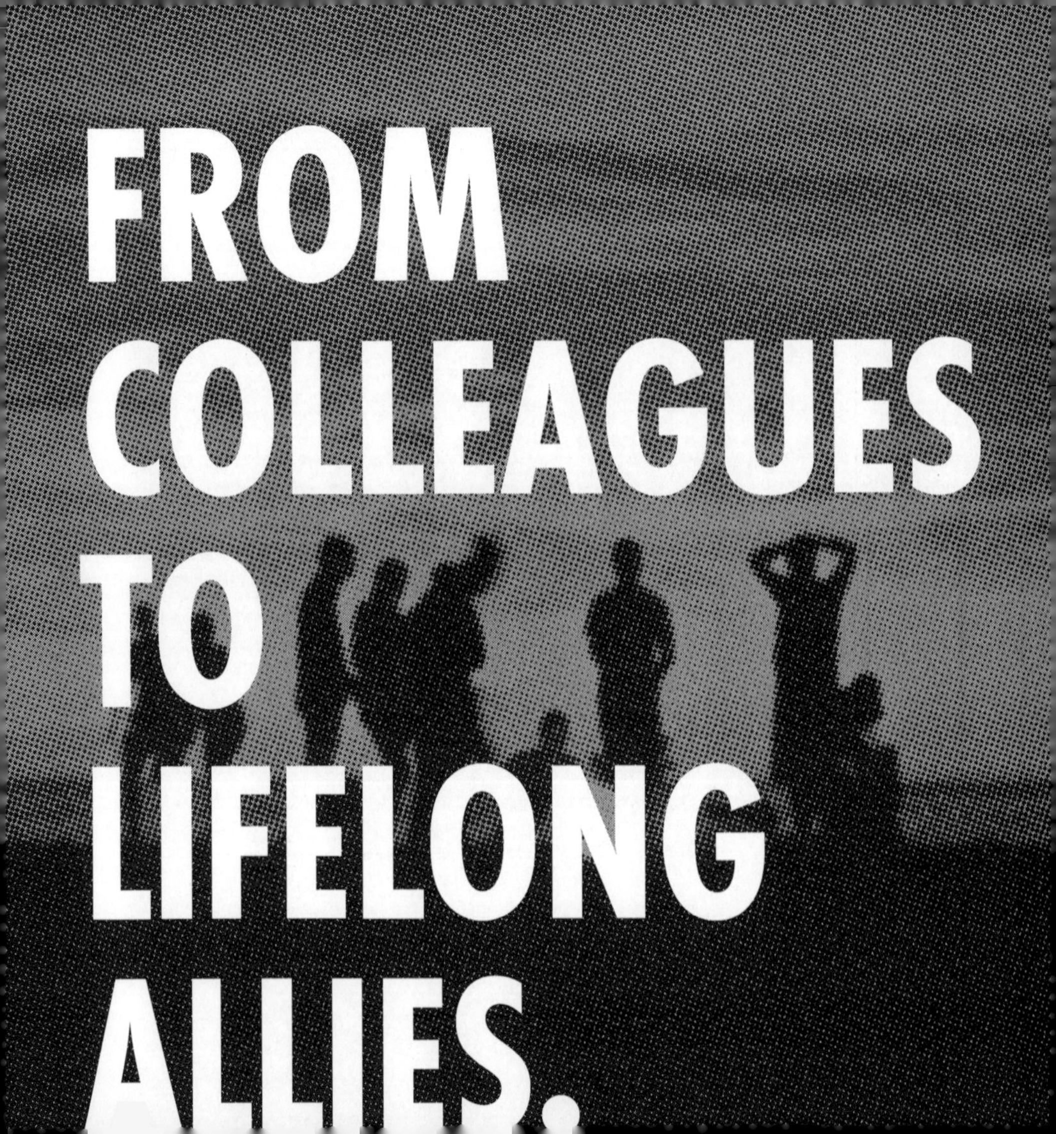
FROM
COLLEAGUES
TO
LIFELONG
ALLIES.

F IS FOR FRIEND-SHIFT

Humans are odd beings – social as well as solitary animals. Friendship brings us not only the mental health benefits of increased connection, it makes us stronger and healthier, too, with proven benefits to our immune system. That's why friendships at work should be encouraged. People with workplace friendships are nearly three times more likely to say they love their companies while people lacking in social support suffer more than others from the effects of work stress. When you're among friends, work that could otherwise be seen as toil or graft can be elevated through the mindful sharing of the task in hand. This resonance brings both energy and the feeling of being part of something greater.

Many of us, however, have been deterred from making meaningful friendships at work for fear of exposing too much of ourselves and being unprofessional. Broken advice from a **Broken Work** model. But surely we're missing something important. The foundation of good business is good relationships built on trust and consistency – the same things you use to make friends: caring, telling the truth, loyalty and, of course, having fun.

Bridging the gap between ourselves and others meets an essential human need for connection.
Find the people who challenge and support you.
Those who are different from you as well as those you get along with easily.
There's always something shared (like values or interests) to spark trust and intimacy.
Why settle for being one person at work and another at play if you can just be you?

'I HAVE NO DUTY TO BE ANYONE'S FRIEND AND NO MAN IN THE WORLD HAS A DUTY TO BE MINE. NO CLAIMS, NO SHADOW OF NECESSITY. FRIENDSHIP IS UNNECESSARY, LIKE PHILOSOPHY, LIKE ART, LIKE THE UNIVERSE ITSELF (FOR GOD DID NOT NEED TO CREATE). IT HAS NO SURVIVAL VALUE; RATHER IT IS ONE OF THOSE THINGS WHICH GIVE VALUE TO SURVIVAL.' CS LEWIS[42]

We can shift our relationships with our co-workers, evolving them from short-term functional colleagues into lasting allies. This extends not just to the people you work alongside on a daily basis but to your customers, suppliers and anyone whose life you touch meaningfully through your work. By writing this book together, we moved from acquaintances to friends, and from friendship to the beginnings of a formidable sustainable business partnership. When we committed to this project, we'd worked with each other only occasionally in the four-year period of our acquaintance. We had in fact only spent four hours alone together. Initially we thought the writing itself would be the difficult task that forged a friendship but, actually, it was a joy to share. Instead, what brought us together was how we supported each other through everything that life threw at us during the writing process. When JP was flat on her back with a ruptured disc, Sara typed (with an amputated finger). When Sara needed space and time to manage a miscarriage, JP picked up the work without hesitation and kept things moving. This level of commitment, compassion and partnership carried us through everything – keeping us writing and working because we were stronger together. Now that's (business) partnership. That's **Friend-shift**.

---

[42] Lewis, CS (1960) *The Four Loves,* reprinted in 2012 by Collins.

TWEAKS FOR YOU

→ Be wary of advice about how dangerous it is to make friends at work – that's the **Broken Work** model that pitches you and your colleagues against each other in a race to climb the ladder.

→ If there is someone you really resonate with, in or outside your organisation, find a common interest or cause and create a way to get involved in a project together. This makes it part of your day job to spend time working hard with them and gives you the opportunity to make the **Friend-shift**.

SHIFTS FOR YOUR TEAM

→ Encourage team members to join professional organisations to grow support networks and friendships in the sector.

→ Create a nurturing and trusted environment that celebrates friendship and open, constructive communication: not just the easy stuff but the hard conversations, too.

JUMPS FOR YOUR ORGANISATION

→ Phase out toxicity and unhealthy competition in the workplace, making sure that success is not achieved at the cost of others.

→ Show vulnerability in your leadership team's style of working, with consistency, openness and humility leading the way. Help your leaders to be **Gentle Warriors** and not **Powercocks**.

FEEL THE
WAY.

G

IS FOR GO WITH THE GOOSEBUMPS

We all know the feeling when we get suddenly hot or cold with fear. It's a leftover of our previous more hairy selves, a fight or flight mechanism that's helped humans survive as we've evolved. We may have less hair today but our sympathetic nervous system still releases a chemical called norepinephrine when we feel extreme emotions or temperatures. Adrenaline then floods our body and stimulates the tiny muscles that literally make our hair stand on end. Some call this the pilomotor reflex. For the rest of us, it's the goosebumps – a pointed reminder from our animal selves that we're getting cold (find shelter; put a jumper on), in danger (run!) or really on to something (oooooh!). Getting sensitive to the goosebumps is key to unlocking your intuition and honing your instincts. Our intuition is, in reality, 'pattern recognition'[43] but there is no use one part of your brain spotting patterns if another part of you is ignoring them. The trick is to trust your gut instinct and pay attention to those goosebumps – they are leading you somewhere good.

Come on, be an animal!
You've been one longer than you've been a worker, so trust your animal instinct.
Tune into the unconscious part of your brain and benefit from its higher capacity and pool of experiences.
Draw on it.
Listen to that inner voice.
Feel your way forwards and channel your inner wisdom.

---

[43] Harari, Yuval Noah (2019) *Twenty One Lessons for the 21st Century*, Vintage.

'CHILLS RAN UP MY ARMS. THE HAIRS ON THE BACK OF MY NECK STOOD UP FOR AN INSTANT, AND I FELT A LITTLE SICK, A LITTLE DIZZY. I FELT LIKE I WAS FALLING IN LOVE, OR HAD JUST HEARD ALARMING NEWS, ALWAYS LOOKING OVER A PRECIPICE AT SOMETHING BEAUTIFUL AND MESMERISING, BUT DANGEROUS ... SUCH AN INTENSE EMOTIONAL AND PHYSIOLOGICAL REACTION DOESN'T STRIKE ME OFTEN, BUT IT HAPPENS ENOUGH (AND IS CONSISTENT ENOUGH WITH SYMPTOMS REPORTED BY PEOPLE ALL OVER THE WORLD, ALL THROUGHOUT HISTORY) THAT I BELIEVE I CAN CONFIDENTLY CALL IT BY ITS NAME: INSPIRATION.' ELIZABETH GILBERT[44]

Anita Roddick talks about how she maintained some 'intimate part herself – the original core, if you like, in a business gone global' by tuning into and using her instinct: 'There are no roadmaps, no instruction manuals. Passion is your guide. Instinct tells you where to go when a challenge arises ... I need to find new ways to push the limits of business, to change its language, to make it a force for positive change.'[45]

You don't need to be the founder or director to put your instinct to work in a way that helps your organisation. Online shoe retailer Zappos encourages its call-centre employees to react in any positive way that enhances the customer experience. Empowering and trusting staff to react as humans and do what feels right has made for some great stories, such as Zappos staff sending flowers to someone who'd lost a relative, talking with customers on the phone for 10 hrs 29 minutes and sending a care package to a soldier customer in Afghanistan.

---

[44] Gilbert, Elizabeth (2016) *Big Magic: Creative Living Beyond Fear,* Bloomsbury.

[45] Roddick, Anita (2000) *Business as Unusual,* Thorsons.

TWEAKS FOR YOU

→ Learn to pay attention: the ideas that give you the goosebumps as you hear them or hear yourself saying them are the good ideas – the ones in which genius and joy lie.

→ Ask yourself if you trust your gut enough to go for it. Be ready to 'tune out' the crowd and 'tune in' to your instinct. Watch what happens when you follow or reject it. Now can you trust your instinct to keep taking you somewhere good?

SHIFTS FOR YOUR TEAM

→ There is no handbook to train people to 'sense things' but you want your team to have a combination of deep knowledge and an intuitive feel for a situation. Talk to them about it and model it where you can.

→ To enable people to **Go with the Goosebumps**, you have to trust them to be able to cope when things go wrong. We have to learn from our mistakes so we can develop and hone our instinct.

JUMPS FOR YOUR ORGANISATION

→ Invite the goosebumps into your organisation by giving people the space and autonomy to work out what feels right. Empower them to act on instinct.

→ Allow space for Anita Roddick-style creative chaos by resisting over-systemisation. People can still benefit from freedom, even in jobs confined by necessity to specific processes and systems.

TACKLE THE HARD STUFF HEAD ON AND EARLY.

H IS FOR HIT IT LIKE A RUGBY PLAYER

When conflict arises or an awkward situation occurs, we often shy away from dealing with it. In many cases, when the response is too weak or late, everyone gets hurt; by trying to ignore it, the situation is likely to worsen. Rugby has a lot to teach us here: if you go hard into a tackle, you're less likely to get injured; it's only when you don't fully commit that you end up with problems. If you **Hit it Like a Rugby Player**, nine times out of 10 you will come off better for having tackled the situation clearly and powerfully in the initial stages. In short, save yourself from unnecessary anguish or the anxiety of a snowballing concern by pre-empting conflict at the outset.

Embrace your Gentle Warrior.
Take confident, clear and direct action.
Be courageous in facing potentially awkward situations.
Don't bury your head in the sand – nip problems in the bud.
It's not about being aggressive but being brave.
The longer you leave a problem or situation, the more it will take out of you in the long run.

'BECAUSE NO MATTER HOW HARD A CONVERSATION IS, I KNOW THAT ON THE OTHER SIDE OF THAT DIFFICULT CONVERSATION LIES PEACE. KNOWLEDGE. AN ANSWER IS DELIVERED. CHARACTER IS REVEALED. TRUCES ARE FORMED. MISUNDERSTANDINGS RESOLVED.' SHONDA RHIMES[46]

When JP was setting up her first business, she would have found it easy on some mornings to retreat under the duvet and hide from the day's challenges and critical decisions. Her partner Nick's encouragement at such times was: 'Hit it like a rugby player!' Since then, JP has shared this piece of advice with the hundreds of female entrepreneurs she has mentored. 'Hitting it!' now forms the basis of being a **Gentle Warrior** – tackling a difficult thing early on, even if you don't want to, for the sake of all involved. When Sara was in one of her leadership roles and being bullied by a **Powercock**, every day at work felt like a battle. She had long since rejected the idea of herself as a fighter. More often than not she ignored her intuition when it told her to fight because she hadn't yet come to appreciate the value of fighting gently. When her mentor, Bertrand Cornaire, advised her to 'take him out', she went in hesitantly at first but the **Powercock** came back stronger and more aggressive. Bertrand immediately identified the problem: 'You have stabbed him and left the knife in: you gave him the weapon! Of course he is coming back to you.' He explained to Sara that she was learning the hard way how conflict and difficulty intensify when you don't tackle problems early on.

---

[46] Rhimes, Shonda (2015) *Year of Yes: How to Dance it Out, Stand in the Sun and Be Your Own Person*, Simon & Schuster.

TWEAKS FOR YOU

→ Keep relationships healthy by dealing with conflict and having the hard conversations early. Be kind and gentle when intervening. When it feels uncomfortable, remember you are working to stop it feeling worse and being more complicated later.

→ Use the **Hit it Like a Rugby Player** approach not just with difficult relationships and situations but with projects, too. Whenever you have a chance and you know what needs doing to move a project forward, get on with it.

SHIFTS FOR YOUR TEAM

→ Work out how much like rugby players you and your team are (in behaviour rather than looks!). Do you tackle things early with the confidence and power to make them successful and safe? Are you **Gentle Warriors** who only use force where necessary? If not, why not?

→ When you know something is wrong in your team or on a project, don't sit on it: be active. Work positively with others on what is needed and get the problem sorted.

JUMPS FOR YOUR ORGANISATION

→ Ensure respectful conflict has a healthy place in your company's culture both internally and externally. Remember: the greater the challenge, the greater the opportunity.

→ If the concept works for you but the phrase doesn't, why not work with your teams to find your own phrase to capture the **Hit it Like a Rugby Player** mentality so you can truly own it?

GIVE AS
YOU
GROW.

I IS FOR IN SERVICE

We honour heroes such as Florence Nightingale or Mahatma Gandhi for their work for others but being a giver isn't only about extraordinary acts of self-sacrifice. Being 'of service' can also be about smaller things, such as connecting people, sharing knowledge, mentoring and championing people and projects. One suggestion is to do pretty much what organisations used to do. After all, the modern concept of businesses 'giving back' has its ancient roots in tithing, where the 'Contribution of net profits into community projects is … a form of giving back into the community, based on the premise that business cannot flourish without the community it serves.'[47] Tadao Yoshida, founder of YKK, called this a 'cycle of goodness' – a company can only survive by coexisting with a community in a two-way process where both business and community are valued and provide for one another.

Have you asked yourself lately what's it all for?
You know – beyond making money or hitting targets.
How you can be In Service.
Where you can ask: 'Who am I doing this for?'
Where you can use your unique 'you-ness' to express yourself and make an impact.
Does that help answer another question?
You know, the biggie.
The 'Why am I here?'

---

[47] Higgins, Polly (2011) *Earth is our Business,* Shepheard-Walwyn.

'THE BEST WAY TO FIND YOURSELF IS TO LOSE YOURSELF IN THE SERVICE OF OTHERS.' MAHATMA GANDHI[48]

The idea of working in the service of others is built into us as human beings. Faith groups and charities have long led the way, both socially and environmentally, but more recently social enterprises have opened up a new discussion about harnessing the power of doing good while being enterprising. At the top of this list is outdoor clothing brand Patagonia, which has addressed environmental and societal problems in every aspect of its work. From a simple commitment to look after staff and the environment[49], the principle of stewardship underpins the founder's efforts to protect and rewild land in his adoptive home of Patagonia. The company's work has also inspired 1% for the Planet, an alliance of businesses that donate at least one per cent of their annual revenues to environmental organisations worldwide.[50]

Both Sara's and JP's work choices have been defined by a desire to make a difference. JP calls this Giving As You Grow, an approach she has applied throughout her career, most notably through Brand Amplifier, a charity she set up and funded through one of her first businesses, JPC. Believing that sharing knowledge inspires others, the charity has helped hundreds of women become the next generation of female entrepreneurs. JPC continues to work closely with its local authority to ensure this support is woven into wider work to generate wealth for local communities. Meanwhile, WorkWild gives three per cent of its turnover to activities that address climate change and the wealth gap – the two critical problems Sara founded WorkWild to address. WorkWild's charitable giving has supported research to help the UK address the climate crisis, helping to build lifeboats and rescue training centres and supporting the provision of affordable workspaces to social and creative entrepreneurs.

---

[48] Commonly attributed to Gandhi, date unknown.

[49] Chouinard, Yvon (2005) *Let My People Go Surfing,* Penguin.

[50] Higgins, Polly (2015) *Eradicating Ecocide,* Shepheard-Walwyn.

TWEAKS FOR YOU

→ How much service do you provide and does it focus on the causes you care about? (Look under X is for '**XXXX it!**' if you're not sure what these are.)

→ Ask yourself if you can afford to work less and volunteer more. If you can, what do you need to do to make that happen?

SHIFTS FOR YOUR TEAM

→ See if there are simple and quick ways your team can build impact and service into its day-to-day work, and help the team work them in.

→ Empower your team members to always be of service to one another.

JUMPS FOR YOUR ORGANISATION

→ Can you shift the definition of success for your organisation from making money to working together to contribute to society?

→ Donate a set percentage of your turnover (not just profit!) to charitable causes or set up your own foundation or charity. Work with your employees to identify what causes they'd like to support and allow their input to shape this giving (for example, by facilitating payroll giving).

SORT STUFF OUT AND LET IT GO.

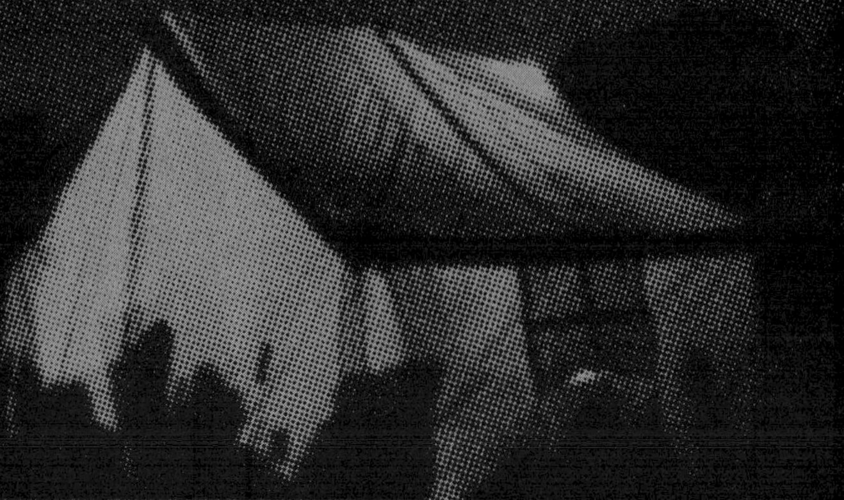

J

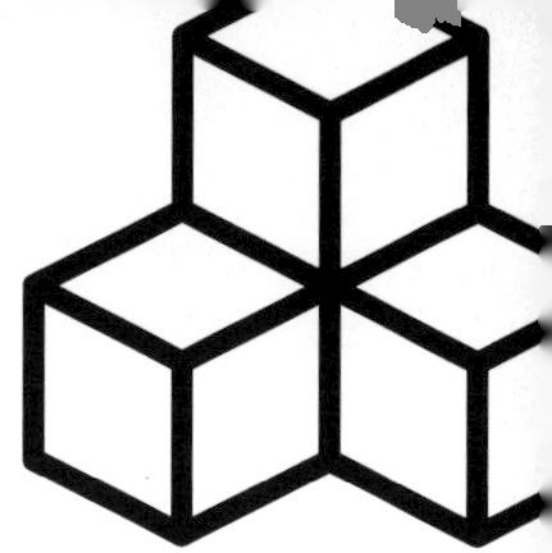

IS FOR JUST WHAT YOU NEED

Roman stoic and philosopher Seneca called private possessions the 'greatest source of human misery'[51] and if you've moved office or home recently, you probably know the truth of this. If you aren't careful, the stuff of work (files, folders, equipment, furniture, copies of reports, etc.) will cost you more to keep than acquire. And it's not just you: in recent years there's been a significant expansion of the storage industry, which is eating up space in our cities and our budgets. When it comes to stuff, less is quite literally more, giving you increased mobility, freedom and the ability to venture further and wider while saving on storage costs.

Stuff takes on a life of its own – slowing you down and distracting you from getting to the important things in life and work.
Liberate yourself by having less baggage – don't break your back carrying it all with you.
Like Mary Poppins, take only what you need – travel light and live light.
Share, sell and recycle. Cut your stuff. Cut your losses.
Taking responsibility for your stuff will set you free.

---

[51] Seneca *On the Shortness of Life* (Penguin edition 2004).

'ODDLY, THE MORE I THREW AWAY, THE MORE I SEEMED TO HAVE.' RACHEL NAOMI REMEN[52]

Decluttering expert Marie Kondo recently tapped into this cultural malaise, sharing her philosophy of tidying and helping people sift through their possessions. But it's not just literal luggage we're talking about: emotional baggage can need looking at too (see L is for **Look in the Shadows** for more on this). As executive coach Nic Crisp says: 'The first step to getting what you want is having the courage to get rid of what you don't.'[53]

As huge fans of camping and boat life, JP and Sara are naturally drawn to small spaces and simplifying stuff. Yet even though JP is well known for travelling with only hand luggage, even on longer adventures lasting a number of weeks, she's still feeling the pain of going through boxes from a big business move several years ago. When she worked at social enterprise workspace Bootstrap, Sara had a small business storage facility and was always astounded by how much companies would pay to store things they no longer used. When talking to the owners of the stored materials, it quickly became clear that they would rather lose money (even at a time of need) than do the tough emotional work of going through the old files.

---

[52] Remen, Rachel Naomi (2006) *The Little Book of Kitchen Table Wisdom,* Riverhead.

[53] Crisp, Nic (2019) *Courage Dear Heart: How to Look Back, Learn and Leap Forward,* independently published.

TWEAKS FOR YOU

→ Hone your work kit to just the things you need and the things that bring you joy. Give away, share, sell or recycle the things you no longer need.

→ Getting rid of paperwork is trickier. Take things one step at a time. Divide and conquer by ditching half of what is easy to lose and putting into a box anything that is harder to let go of. Come back a month later and have another go. Purge and reduce until you are done.

SHIFTS FOR YOUR TEAM

→ Refine your team's kit to reduce your overheads (by saving money on storage) and create a calmer work environment.

→ Burn, baby, burn! How about a campfire with the team if you've got lots of paperwork to get rid of? Read things aloud and let the memories and conversations unfurl. You'll be surprised how many unshared pieces of good news and horror stories come out. There are few things as cathartic – or indeed as intimate and bonding – as a good campfire.

JUMPS FOR YOUR ORGANISATION

→ Look at your workspace – how much space are you taking up and paying rent for? What furniture, equipment, paperwork and other kit do you have? Are you wasting good money that could be spent elsewhere? If so, start ditching things now or pass them on.

→ Can you share more with other organisations, source second-hand items or Freecycle them when you have too many? Become part of the real sharing economy and pass it on!

GET (SH)IT
DONE!

K

IS FOR KNUCKLE DOWN

There are times when we all need to throw everything at a task to get it done. Often, once you've knuckled down to the hard graft, you get a great sense of achievement and can end on a high. You need to be careful, of course: pulling an occasional all-nighter is one thing but you can't do that every day. And it's best not to. Relying on adrenaline to get you through will make you stressed and/or ill. Not to mention difficult to be around. However, when you do **Knuckle Down** alone or as a team you often grow so much it's hard to believe what you've been able to produce. Working hard can generate huge growth in skills. The trick is to know when to **Knuckle Down** and when not to. Check out D is for **Do or Do Not** for help in making choices and, if you firmly believe you need to **Knuckle Down** after that, read on here.

Stick your music on.
Set a timer and get some pizza in.
Push it real hard.
Keep at it until you hit that deadline, crack that problem.
Find your flow. And just get it done.
Knowing you have what it takes to see it through is a good thing.

'HOW OFTEN IN LIFE WE COMPLETE A TASK THAT WAS BEYOND THE CAPABILITY OF THE PERSON WE WERE WHEN WE FIRST STARTED.' ROBERT BRAULT[54]

The phrase **Knuckle Down** comes from the game of marbles. It's a move in which a player holds the marble by their crooked index finger and flicks it with their thumb. Yes, we'd all rather be playing marbles but surely we can squeeze some fun out of a task that simply can't be put off any longer? If possible, find joy in the flow or, at the very least, in the pleasure of getting something done.

When starting out in our careers, we were prone to overwork and too many nights in the 90s and noughties were spent sleeping under desks. We're not proud of that but it taught us we needed a better way of doing things. Knuckling down cannot be a permanent state of being. Now we only **Knuckle Down** when we know a project needs it and when we can enjoy harnessing our passion and energy to get it done. It may well be the same for you. Remember that this is just a stage in your energetic cycle – you are knuckling down when you need to and nurturing yourself in between the bouts of intensity.

---

[54] Brault, Robert (2014) *Round Up the Usual Subjects,* CreateSpace.

TWEAKS FOR YOU

→ Think back on times when you've knuckled down: what was your energy like and how can you capture and cultivate that kind of energy again? Do you need to rest more or play more to get inspired and be able to **Knuckle Down** next time you need to?

→ Try unearthing your curiosity and creativity by doodling, mindmapping or writing stream-of-consciousness pages as recommended in *The Artist's Way*[55].

SHIFTS FOR YOUR TEAM

→ Keep meetings short and, where possible, use sprints (short bursts of working together) to **Knuckle Down** on a focused task. There's no use being in meetings all day if you then have to **Knuckle Down** after hours to get the actions done.

→ Establish healthy expectations and help your team ditch the guilt. Ensure everyone knows you value people knuckling down when needed but it isn't expected all the time.

JUMPS FOR YOUR ORGANISATION

→ Do you honestly have enough people to do the work? If not, can you ensure no one is having to **Knuckle Down** too much and too often? Can you redefine what hard work means to your organisation – shifting from long hours to shorter, focused bursts?

→ Take you leadership team away from distractions for a proper chunk of time to focus and resolve things that would otherwise take weeks of back-and-forth emailing and miscommunication.

---

[55] Cameron, Julia (1991) *The Artist's Way*, Macmillan.

LET'S NOT BE TODDLERS AT WORK ANY MORE.

L

IS FOR LOOK IN THE SHADOWS

Managing immature emotions at work is exhausting. We've all come across toddlers in the workplace – not cute, real toddlers, of course, but the intrusive toddler-selves we revert to when the going gets tough. They get in the way of the work and hang out in the workplace because the grown-ups there need to **Look in the Shadows**. We were all toddlers (real ones) once, and all have shadow-selves, made of the parts of ourselves we have ignored or hidden in order to present a more pleasing 'self' to the world. Shadow work is about accepting everything about ourselves that, for whatever reason, we have previously suppressed, submerged and pushed down into darkness. It's down to us all, then, to seek our shadow-selves through self-development or therapy – to find, listen to and give comfort to our toddler-self. Only then can we accept our shadows as part of who we are and celebrate ourselves as whole and lovable. Shadow work is deep and personal, allowing us to live from a place of wholeness and expansion, and it might well be the most important work you'll ever do.

What is it that sets you off into toddler mode?
Who is throwing their toys out of the pram?
Hiding the ugly stuff, the painful stuff, the truth of how we feel.
Are the bits that bother you in others really the disowned bits of yourself?
Unpick the unhelpful narratives you absorbed (often in childhood).
Remember, the older we get, the harder our shadow-selves are to keep hidden or to deny.

'EVERYTHING WITH SUBSTANCE CASTS A SHADOW. THE EGO STANDS TO THE SHADOW AS LIGHT TO SHADE. THIS IS THE QUALITY THAT MAKES US HUMAN. MUCH AS WE WOULD LIKE TO DENY IT, WE ARE IMPERFECT. AND PERHAPS IT IS IN WHAT WE DON'T ACCEPT ABOUT OURSELVES – OUR AGGRESSION AND SHAME, OUR GUILT AND PAIN – THAT WE DISCOVER OUR HUMANITY.' CONNIE ZWEIG AND JEREMIAH ABRAMS[56]

We all know what it's like in the workplace when the pressure is on and someone (perhaps even you?) is being immature. 'Don't set them off, you know what they're like, they're in one of those moods. We're all treading on eggshells.' Bringing your toddler-self to work or, worse still, having to put up with the toddler-selves of others won't just impede productivity; it will tear you, your team and your workplace apart. When someone at work kicks off or bothers you, they'll be triggering your trauma before you know it, while your response will trigger theirs. And so it continues, with everyone pushing everyone else's buttons in a workplace-turned-pre-school where no one can get anything done.

The ancient Greeks recognised the need to honour all of the parts of the self – so much so they worshipped all the light and dark elements of humanity as omnipotent gods and goddesses. The Greeks knew that if a mortal ignored the deities, such an action would invite those immortals to turn against and ultimately destroy that person. That sense of recognising and respecting the whole self is one that continues through into Western therapeutic practice. Much later, psychiatrist and psychoanalyst Carl Jung (incidentally also an artist, craftsman and builder – now those are a few side hustles) honoured the shadow in his work. Jung refused to see people in need of therapy as ill, sick or broken and encouraged them to explore and befriend their shadows and give them what they need most – light.

---

[56] Zweig, Connie and Abrams, Jeremiah (1991) *Meeting the Shadow: the Hidden Power of the Dark Side of Human Nature,* Penguin.

TWEAKS FOR YOU

→ Keep a journal. Write whatever you like – it can't be wrong and it can help you to recognise and express how you feel and to spot patterns. Rather than turning off bad feelings and emotions, sit with them and be curious about them.

→ Practise letting things go. Work with a qualified therapist to understand yourself better, talk to friends or explore ancient philosophies as ways to loosen the grip on negative emotions.

SHIFTS FOR YOUR TEAM

→ Revisit the attitudes for **Working Wild** given in this book with your team and see if you can find one attitude to celebrate and one for everyone to work on.

→ Open up a conversation with members of your team about where their **Broken Work** attitudes come from. What impact do they have and is there a desire for change? How can you work together with compassion to unlearn some of them?

JUMPS FOR YOUR ORGANISATION

→ Rethink training and send people on exploratory journeys that help them work on themselves and, in doing so, help your people to be their best – freed from their worst behaviours and destructive habits.

→ Build a positive mental health culture throughout your organisation, for example, by making therapy something that is actively recommended or by providing a space in which to meditate.

GET
SERIOUS
ABOUT
HAVING FUN.

M

IS FOR MESS ABOUT

Who has ever complained that something's too much fun? Yet how often do we give ourselves time and space to **Mess About** and enjoy ourselves? While duties and obligations can erode our natural spontaneity, it's precisely that positive energy which brings us true wildness, true joy. Tantra suggests that if we are too cultured and curated in our (work) lives, we risk losing all that is natural by becoming 'a mechanical thing, not floating, not flowing.'[57] Instead, playing and messing about can help us to resist and break out of structures and 'live moment to moment, live with alertness'.

This sounds like good advice to us. This is where we can take a break from structure, order, rules, obligations and pressure to be productive. Let's 'appreciate the virtues of the messy – the untidy, unquantified, uncoordinated, improvised, imperfect, incoherent, crude, cluttered, random, ambiguous, vague, difficult, diverse or even dirty'[58] joy of messing around.

To have fun is to succeed.
You can't force fun and you certainly can't organise it. That's like explaining a joke.
Booring!
Face it: it's both pointless and absolutely necessary to mess around.

---

[57] Osho (1975) *Tantra,* Rajneesh Foundation.

[58] Harford, Tim (2016) *Messy: How to be Creative and Resilient in a Tidy-Minded World,* Little, Brown Book Group.

'I THINK YOU SHOULD TAKE YOUR JOB SERIOUSLY, BUT NOT YOURSELF – THAT IS THE BEST COMBINATION.' DAME JUDI DENCH[59]

In his book *How to be Free,* Tom Hodgkinson calls out the absurdity of our self-created universe and the 'essential nothingness at the heart of man'. He describes the 'mind-forged' shackles of anxiety, fear, mortgages, money, guilt, debt, governments, boredom, supermarkets, bills, melancholy, pain, depression and waste as the 'enemies of freedom.'[60] If he's right, we all have a playful duty to reclaim our rightful nothingness by freeing ourselves from those shackles. (Of course, it is a lot easier to **Mess About** when you are not worrying about money. So if your financial situation is holding you back, check out S is for **Survive**.)

In the sea one day, Sara struck up conversation with a swimmer who seemed very healthy and young for his age. When she asked his advice on staying youthful, he replied: 'Swim a lot in the sea and mess about.' Great advice indeed. JP and Sara certainly both love water (messing about in and on it) but that's not where the play stops: it's no coincidence that JP's fancy-dress boxes are the source of many an outfit for friends and parties and that, at one point, Sara had more dressing-up costumes than normal clothes! Maybe swimming and dressing up aren't your things but messing about certainly should be.

---

[59] Dench, Judi (2012) *And Furthermore,* W&N.

[60] Hodgkinson, Tom (2007) *How to be Free,* Penguin.

TWEAKS FOR YOU

→ Keep some 'baggy time' in your schedule for messing about every day (at least 10 minutes). When you've managed 10 minutes, scale up to ring-fence some playfulness and play until you've got an hour or two for something pointless (that you love) in your life every week.

→ Find two or three friends (or colleagues you'd like to become friends) and set aside some time for doing something totally pointless and fun together.

SHIFTS FOR YOUR TEAM

→ Schedule an hour or two once a quarter for the whole team to **Mess About**. Resist playing the hierarchy card. Don't spoil the fun by having grand expectations of it improving innovation or increasing bonding. Just **Mess About**.

→ Systemise spontaneity. Plan unstructured time for working together when you can **Mess About** on project ideas. Start with a one-hour chat and see where it goes. You may strike gold, you may not.

JUMPS FOR YOUR ORGANISATION

→ Protect your team's time off by policing overwork and committing to paying your people properly. With their own time and resources freed up, they will sort out the messing about themselves.

→ If you don't like the idea of your employees needing time beyond work to **Mess About**, have a look at ordering some robots (we hear they are really coming on!) ;)

REWILD
YOURSELF.

N

IS FOR NAUGHTY AND NAKED

Nakedness = honesty = truth. We arrive in this world naked and, when we leave, we take nothing to remind us of our stay. Little wonder, then, that rewilding the self starts with getting naked. Don't worry if you're shy: you don't need to take everything off. Just shedding your footwear can be enough – walking around barefoot not only makes you feel young again but makes your brain young again. 'Shoes are to feet what a blindfold is to the eyes'[61] and 'Going shoeless is now recognized as an anti-Alzheimer's, brain-boosting activity because the sole sensation entices your brain into growing extra, efficient neuron connections.'[62] Then there are the cultural as well as scientific benefits of getting naked: the empowerment that comes with reclaiming our true bodies. Not the curated, online images of ourselves – the false personae that distance us ever more from ourselves, let alone others – but the raw, natural bodies we refuse to despise.

Here just for that moment between our birth and our death.
Why not be as natural as we can in the middle?
For our true nature to shine through, we need to strip bare.
We all long for radiance, for laughter.
The will for mischief and to have a bloody good time.
Who really needs or wants to be a goody two-shoes?
When we're born to be wild.

---

[61] Cregan-Reid, Vybarr (2018) *How the World We Made is Remaking Us,* Cassell.

[62] Doidge, Norman (2015) *The Brain's Way of Healing,* Allen Lane.

'I WAS, IN FACT, HOMESICK FOR WILDNESS, AND WHEN I FOUND IT I KNEW HOW INTIMATELY – HOW RESONANTLY – I BELONGED THERE. WE ARE CHARGED WITH THIS. ALL OF US. FOR THE HUMAN SPIRIT HAS A PRIMAL ALLEGIANCE TO WILDNESS, TO REALLY LIVE, TO SNATCH THE FRUIT AND TO SUCK IT, TO SPILL THE JUICE. WE MAY THINK WE ARE DOMESTICATED BUT WE ARE NOT.' JAY GRIFFITHS[63]

Although lots of us are practising wildness independently, alone or with others – such as by wild camping or wild swimming – few workplaces afford us the opportunity to get naked (in the nicest possible sense of the word) while we work. Sara was lucky enough to find her way to one of them, Working Wild for a year at the Centre for Alternative Technology in Powys, mid-Wales. As the duty manager of a seven-acre visitor site bursting with wild places for the team to roam, Sara was outside every day, returning to the office only to do admin or because she was forced to by changes in the weather or her energy levels. The site had a wood-fired sauna and a reservoir, and on many evenings and early mornings she and her colleagues would gather wood, climb the hill and get naked for a swim and relax. Open chats and smiling faces under the stars – what better environment could there be for getting back in touch with a slower rhythm of life and a more honest and open way of working together? Swedish saunas often display signs with the legend: *'In sauna veritas'* (in the sauna, truth prevails) and naked saunas were a huge part of life for Roman senators. A naked conversation is seen as an honest one, capable of cutting to the heart of a serious matter.

---

[63] Griffiths, Jay (2006) *Wild: an Elemental Journey,* Penguin.

TWEAKS FOR YOU

→ Identify the one thing at work that stops you listening to the yearnings of your deepest natural self.

→ What small or critical changes – being more honest, making time for lunch, getting outside more or drinking water – can you make at work to align your work and natural self?

SHIFTS FOR YOUR TEAM

→ Let your people be naughty when it's right for them or the work – encourage them to go through fences, question and be curious.

→ Embrace your team's humanity, working with team members and managers to decide how much inner wild (frail humanity) can be revealed safely at work. Apply this not just to your workplace but to your customers and clients.

JUMPS FOR YOUR ORGANISATION

→ Help your team work to the seasons and feel the rhythms of nature. For example, JPC has bought and planted a tree for every member of its team over 20 years of operating as an organisation.

→ Follow WorkWild's example by saving up for a foundation or a forest – buying up land for rewilding and locking it out of private ownership using solid governance structures.

GET UNDER
A BLUE SKY
AND THINK.

O

IS FOR OUT THERE

Reports say that children should be outside for four to six hours a day. But what about the grown-ups? Most working environments make it difficult, if not impossible, to experience nature in any form. Getting away from an often stagnant work environment, be it an office, classroom or factory floor, has huge health benefits. Escaping from air-conditioned and artificially lit spaces reduces stress and is essential in our quest to reconnect with nature. Too many of us are losing our connection to the cyclical nature of life and time. Getting **Out There** is the only way to reverse this.

To be Out There is to be connected to nature and the natural world.
Wild of heart.
Get Out There also in your thinking.
Be wild of mind.
Embrace radical thinking, alternative and non-linear approaches.
Walk away from your desk and out of the meeting room and meet yourself outdoors.

'WHEN THE MIND IS ENTANGLED, IT IS NICE TO WALK BY THE SEASHORE, TO LET THE RHYTHM OF THE OCEAN INSIDE YOU. THE OCEAN DISENTANGLES THE ... MIND. EVERYTHING LOOSENS AND COMES BACK TO ITSELF. THE FALSE DIVISIONS ARE RELIEVED, RELEASED AND HEALED.' JOHN O'DONOHUE[64]

The human need to go outside to reset ourselves is as old as time. Author and therapist LR Heartsong describes his compulsion to get **Out There** when he feels the 'modern day amnesia' creeping over him as a 'restlessness under my skin, the wild soul, urges me back out into the trees … where I wake up again and remember. Rewilding myself.'[65] Many of us feel like this when our senses are dulling and we seem to lose 'the full, non-domesticated, sensual wildness' of who we are. This concept is echoed by poet and philosopher John O'Donohue in *Anam Cara,* where he writes of how 'the ancient psyche was never as isolated and disconnected as the modern psyche' and suggests this connection was 'informed by mindful, reverent attention to landscape'. Get **Out There** to shake off that **Powercock,** remember your place in the world and be humbled. You are the universe and the universe is in you.

Sylvia, JP's mum, was a **Gentle Warrior** if ever there was one. She had a love of the mountains, a passion for the great outdoors and the first hint of a spring daffodil always put a skip in her step. In the last months of Sylvia's life in and out of hospital, JP and family would visualise with her the memories of long walks on rugged Welsh coastal pathways. Sylvia's desire to be **Out There** was so great, so raw and so human – the essential desire to feel the sun on her face and the wind in her hair. Her incredible strength, power and desire and her elemental need to be surrounded by nature one last time.

---

[64] O'Donohue, John (1999) *Anam Cara: Spiritual Wisdom from the Celtic World,* Bantam.

[65] Heartsong, LR (2018) *To Kneel and Kiss the Earth: Inspiration from the Soul Artist Journal,* Hearthside Press.

TWEAKS FOR YOU

→ Get outside and into wild open spaces as often as you can to touch life and feel the elements. Finding a way to feel the power of the weather is sure to put your day in perspective.

→ Make the most of your commute (however long or short) if you can't get out to a truly wild space. Can you walk the first or last bit and use it as a walking meditation? Observe the small details you might normally rush past and allow yourself to engage and connect with them. Feel the weather, watch the seasons.

SHIFTS FOR YOUR TEAM

→ Outside lunches can be the norm if you make them happen. Start with one or two a month, getting the whole team outside and together in a more natural environment.

→ Could you relocate your team to the beach or the mountains for a short change of scenery? How could you make this work around families and childcare?

JUMPS FOR YOUR ORGANISATION

→ Can you shift from working from home to working **Out There** on a regular basis? Allowing staff to get **Out There** while getting things done can benefit the organisation as well as the employees: they'll feel refreshed and you'll reduce the space you need to rent.

→ With the financial savings gained from reduced floorspace, can you relocate your premises near a park/river/open space to further recharge your workers?

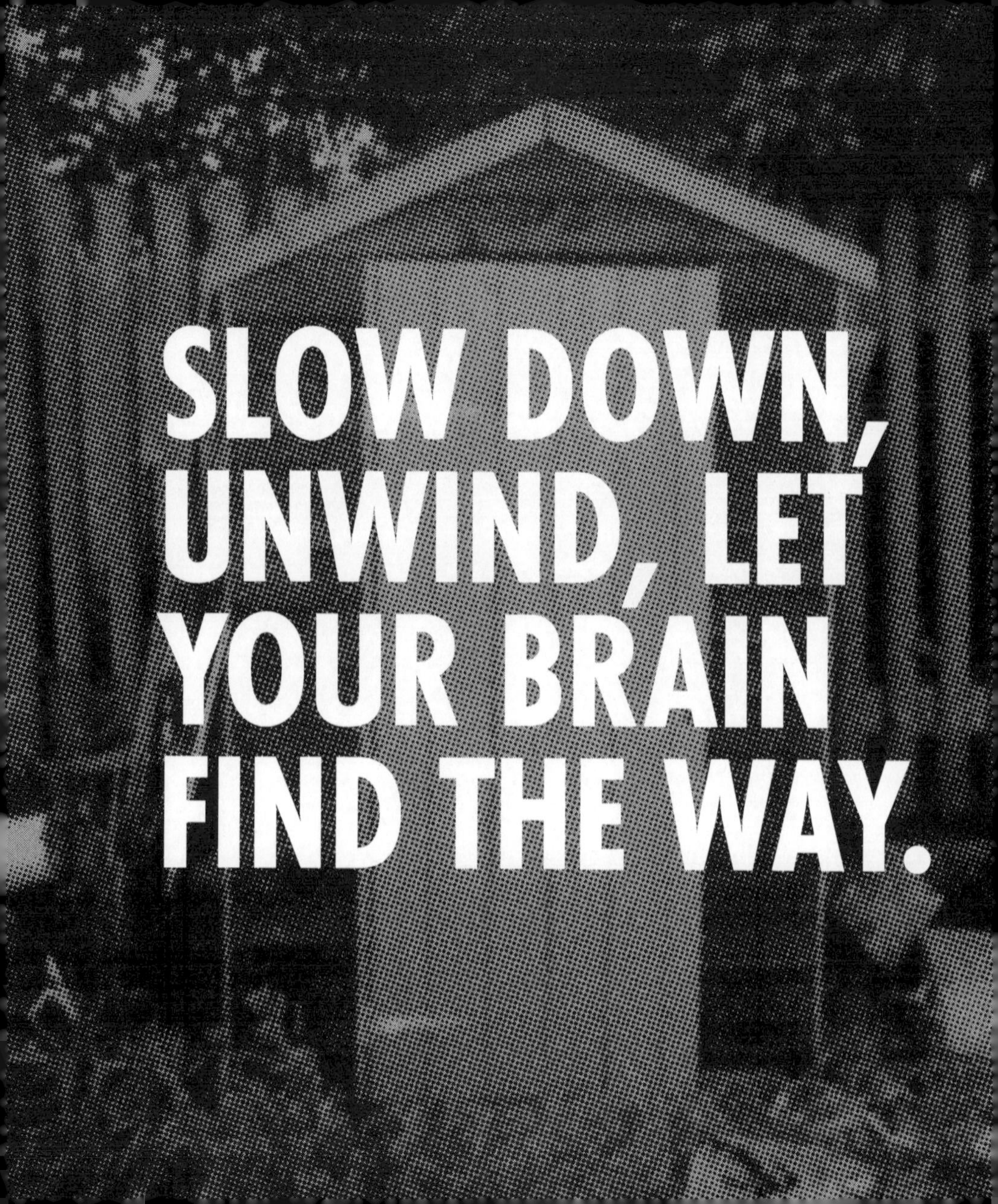
SLOW DOWN, UNWIND, LET YOUR BRAIN FIND THE WAY.

P

IS FOR POTTER AND PERCOLATE

This tool is the equal and opposite of **Knuckle Down**. It's the equivalent of hoeing and tilling soil in a garden or sweeping a stage – the preparation for the main event. The bit where you aren't pushing to hit a deadline or ticking something off a to-do list. This is where you let something be filtered and processed at the back of your mind while you let yourself get on with whatever takes your fancy.

Whatever you're doing, you are enjoying it and are feeling your way to the tasks that bring you joy.

Put your to-do list away.
Let your ideas steep like a pot of tea while you get on with something else.
Use your hands, use your legs. Follow your smile.
Go at a gentle pace.
Linger long on tasks you enjoy and go slow with no expectations of outputs.
Let it be.
Sit on that idea or decision and let the right answer come.
There's no need to rush, it will come to you from deep within.

'I DISCOVERED THAT I COULD SET MY SUBCONSCIOUS MIND TO WORK ON A SPECIFIC TASK WHILE MY CONSCIOUS MIND WAS OCCUPIED WITH PERFORMING WORKDAY RITUALS ... WHEN MY HOSPITAL SHIFT FINISHED I FOUND THAT I COULD GO HOME AND WRITE PAGES AND PAGES, WHILE IN CONTRAST SITTING IN FRONT OF THE COMPUTER FOR HOURS BEFORE WORK HAD YIELDED NOTHING.' HOPE JAHREN[66]

When you **Potter and Percolate**, it's quite likely your brain is taking the opportunity to process something difficult. 'While we are paying close attention to one project, we may be unconsciously processing another,' says economist and journalist Tim Harford.[67] Even simply daydreaming can be 'a powerful way to unlock fresh thoughts'.

Both Sara and JP tend towards speed (and haste?) and the people around us have grown used to (or perhaps bored by) our 'busyness'. Being too busy can prevent you from getting down to the important tasks of reflecting and preparing. By rewilding ourselves in an effort to end our fast and furious ways, we've realised the value of letting things settle and mulling them over. By starting to shift gear a little and slow down, we've been changed by the process. It's fair to say JP's on a steep learning curve with this one but she has learned from those around her who prefer to 'let things soak'. Sara has embraced pottering and is losing her feelings of guilt while enjoying the benefits of a tidier brain and a slower, kinder pace of work. However, getting into the tidying zone has sometimes made her late for work.

---

[66] Jahren, Hope (2017) *Lab Girl: a Story of Trees, Science and Love,* Fleet.

[67] Harford, Tim (2016), *Messy: How to be Creative and Resilient in a Tidy Minded World,* Little, Brown Book Group.

TWEAKS FOR YOU

→ Sometimes allow yourself to ignore your to-do list. Permit yourself time for tidying up or doing the things that seem right. Often you'll find you've achieved more than you would have done by forcing yourself to tick things off that list.

→ If you've a hard problem to crack, set your brain on it but put your fingers to a repetitive task, such as gardening, knitting, washing up or tidying a desk. Trust that your brain will be doing the hard work of unlocking the problem while your body gets on with something else.

SHIFTS FOR YOUR TEAM

→ Make sure your team members don't feel guilty when they potter. Help them find a healthy balance between the 'push it, push it' of knuckling down and the restorative, preparatory actions of pottering.

→ When your team members reach a difficult part of a project or have to make a hard decision, give them time to percolate by sharing thoughts, sleeping on it and regrouping. If it needs to be done that day, at the very least give yourselves half an hour of pottering and talking it through before coming to a decision.

JUMPS FOR YOUR ORGANISATION

→ Make it a rule that you sleep on difficult problems. This gives you time to percolate and let the big ideas, emotions and pressure settle.

→ By all means judge people on their outputs – your organisation needs to get stuff done – but remember the value of pottering and create space for everyone at all levels to feel able to potter as part of their process.

MOVE YOUR
BODY,
MOVE YOUR
MIND.

Q

IS FOR QUESTION OF SPORT

They say sedentary working is the new smoking. The way many of us work at desks is reshaping and damaging our bodies, with back pain – specifically lower-back pain – now the most common reason for missed days of work. Using a standing desk can help you start to turn things around but we need to go further by bringing sport and movement into work. Our bodies crave to do things they recognise as simulations of hunting and gathering (the outdoor activities our bodies evolved to carry out).[68] So why not make space for intense bursts of movement that can help us to balance body and mind and give us what we need to be effective, healthy and happy? There are also group benefits to exercising at the office. While exercise can help improve our mental health (raising your heart rate increases oxygen flow to the parts of your brain that control memory and thinking) as well as physical health, trying new things together with others can help us update our own self-image, draw us closer to each other, help us feel part of something bigger and help us to be brave.[69] Quite simply, those who work out together, work better together.

Don't let your mind, your creativity or your body get stiff.
Shake out the stasis of stodgy ideas and sedentariness.
Move your body, breathe deeply, get that heart going.
Let the blood bring you oxygen and ideas.

---

[68] Cregan-Reid, Vybarr (2018) *Primate Change: How the World We Made is Remaking Us,* Cassell.

[69] McGonigal, Kelly (2019), *The Joy of Movement,* Avery.

'THROUGHOUT HUMAN HISTORY, MOVEMENT – WHETHER LABOUR, RITUAL OR PLAY – HAS HELPED US TO CONNECT, COLLABORATE AND CELEBRATE. TODAY, PHYSICAL ACTIVITY CONTINUES TO DRAW US TOGETHER ... THE JOY OF MOVEMENT IS ACTUALLY THE JOY OF CONNECTION.' KELLY MCGONIGAL

Both of us began our careers in the theatre, so we are no strangers to a warm-up or improv game. While working with multinational clients at Arup to design sustainable buildings and cities, Sara drew on her theatre experience to create workshops using games as ice-breakers. Since then we have brought similar games to WorkWild workshops and our work with new groups of people. For example, the 100 Club is a quick exercise you can do by yourself or with a group. It involves a set of 10 lots of 10 exercises (push ups, jumps, hops, stretches, squats – whatever gets the blood flowing). Done with a group, and often as a surprise in the middle of a very formal meeting, the 100 Club breaks down boundaries, changes the rhythm and invariably ends in laughter. Einstein called this 'combinatory play' or 'the act of opening up one mental channel by dabbling in another'. This is why he would often play the violin when he was having difficulty solving a mathematical puzzle.[70]

Integrating movement into our work routine has helped us shake things up, get problem-solving juices flowing and a sense of togetherness going (see also O is for **Out There** or M is for **Mess About**). We use it all the time in the work we do, whether alone or with others, and neither of us can imagine a working day without it. For the Japanese, too, exercise is part of their daily work routine. Japan helped to lift its economy out of the ruins of World War II with mandatory callisthenics in playgrounds. This filtered through to the offices and many Japanese companies continue to incorporate exercise into their work routines today, understanding that the physical and mental health of their employees has a direct impact on their well-being and productivity.

---

[70] Gilbert, Elizabeth (2016) *Big Magic: Creative Living Beyond Fear*, Bloomsbury.

TWEAKS FOR YOU

→ Remember your body isn't designed for modern-day work, especially if you have to sit at a desk or stand on a door for long hours. Look for ways to integrate a range of movements into your day to reduce the stress on your body, mind and soul.

→ When you get stuck (either at your desk or on a project), try a quick 100 Club as a way to get things going and ideas and energy flowing. If you don't feel comfortable doing this at work, ask yourself what rules and expectations might need to be challenged to make it more normal for you to look after your body and mind during the working day.

SHIFTS FOR YOUR TEAM

→ Provide standing desks and let staff have access to meeting rooms to share exercise activities, such as yoga, in their free time.

→ Encourage everyone to reach beyond their physical inhibitions in the workplace. Moving your body is one of the most natural things. Create your own version of the 100 Club, a dance-off perhaps? If it gets the blood flowing and feels good, it will benefit everyone.

JUMPS FOR YOUR ORGANISATION

→ Rather than sitting still, turn your meeting into a 'walk and talk', an idea Claire Ellis developed for one of JP's companies, JPC, when it moved its London office next to a park.

→ Offer headsets so people can walk and talk on conference calls. If you have a lot of this happening, consider following Procter & Gamble's lead by marking out an indoor and outdoor circuit for people to follow and make being active part of the way your organisation operates.

DO THE RIGHT
THING AND
APOLOGISE
LATER.

R IS FOR REBEL REBEL

Be brave enough to take action, often against the rules or accepted norms. Environmental activist Vandana Shiva talks of our 'moral imperative to rebel' when an accepted system is driving terrible outcomes. Shiva trained as a climate lawyer for the United Nations and is now rebelling 'against a system that is driving extinction, exterminating species and cultures.'[71] Like so many of us, she realised she couldn't make radical enough change while working within the system. A rebellious spirit can spur you into action and liberate you from the helplessness you can feel when facing huge structural problems, vested interests and inertia.

Of course, you don't have to restrict your rebellion to climate change. The whole kit and kaboodle of the way we live and work needs a reboot so gather round a great idea or develop your own. When we say rebel, we don't mean smoking round the back of the bike sheds. We mean doing the right thing to challenge the status quo, and apologising later.

Be a rebel with a cause.
Trust and follow your passion; be brave and act on your beliefs.
Draw on your wild spirit and question anything that seeks to limit it.
Get up when support is needed.
Stand up when it counts.
The only real limit to your rebellion is getting on with it.

---

[71] Extinction Rebellion (2019) *This is Not a Drill: an Extinction Rebellion Handbook,* Penguin.

'WE CAN'T SAVE THE WORLD BY PLAYING BY THE RULES. BECAUSE THE RULES HAVE TO BE CHANGED. EVERYTHING NEEDS TO CHANGE. AND IT HAS TO START TODAY ... IT IS TIME TO REBEL.' GRETA THUNBERG[72]

Co-forming the Ugli community, one of London's most creative and affordable workspace campuses back in 2010, was one of JP's most rebellious business ventures. In the aftermath of the 2008 financial crash, people were angry and sick of being falsely marketed to. The upcycled 120,000 sq foot building was Ugli by name and ugly by nature. With a battle cry of 'We're Ugli, you could be too,' the frank and honest mission pulled together a rich community of creative, forward-thinking businesses and drew them around the core ideas of being super resourceful, more agile, ethical, socially responsible and environmentally conscious. Within six months Ugli was a movement with 750 members running 65 businesses.

---

[72] Thunberg, Greta (2019) *No One is Too Small to Make a Difference,* Penguin.

TWEAKS FOR YOU

→ Find your inner activist and join the rebellion – not necessarily with placards and banners but by doing the right thing, even if that isn't in the rule book (yet).

→ Nurture your wilder rebel self. Work first on your awareness to really get to know yourself and what you stand for, fire up your imagination with your dreams of a better world and commit to following through with action.

SHIFTS FOR YOUR TEAM

→ Work out together what's stopping you, restricting your growth or stifling your humanity at work. Ask yourselves if you feel strongly enough about challenging this to risk rebellion.

→ Once you've identified the thing to rebel against as a team (be it internal or external), you have your rebel purpose! Make a plan and gently get on with changing your world.

JUMPS FOR YOUR ORGANISATION

→ Join us and rebel against the world of **Broken Work** by creating an organisation that is better off **Working Wild**.

→ Encourage activism where possible, reviewing contracts at the very least so they don't stop your people engaging in activism. If a particular cause is important to your organisation, consider giving your employees time off to protest or offer to cover court fees, as Patagonia has done.

KNOW YOUR NEEDS.

S

IS FOR SURVIVE

We each start life from a unique place with access to different skills, budgets, networks and resources. We all have different financial needs (both to cover overheads and to bring joy) and responsibilities to partners, family and friends. While our paths have different starting points, don't we all deserve to reach that special place where our true needs are understood and met – to live 'the good life'?

Professor of psychology Keith Payne describes poverty as being like gravity because to overcome poverty, individuals need to reach 'escape velocity'. Poverty can shorten your life by significantly affecting your physical and mental health. At the same time, thinking you are poor has been found to be as damaging to your health as actually being poor.[73] So it's time to evolve your economy – not just to get by, but to find freedom and security.

Battling to make ends meet.
The stress, the fear and the heartache of barely surviving.
Struggling to keep up with others.
Needing to be better, different, somehow more.
Just knowing what is enough and being able to get it. To enjoy it.
That is survival.

---

[73] Payne, Keith (2017) *The Broken Ladder: How Inequality Changes the Way We Think, Live and Die*, W&N.

'THAT TIGHT FEELING HITS YOUR CHEST, YOUR BREATHING GETS A LITTLE SHALLOW ... THOSE LITTLE STRESS DAGGERS ARE ACTUALLY THE SAME QUESTION ON REPEAT: CAN I AFFORD THIS? AND THIS CAN BE AS SMALL AS LUNCH OUT WITH FRIENDS, ALL THE WAY UP TO RETIREMENT.' JESSE MEECHAM[74]

Survival Materialism – a term coined by psychologist Oliver James[75] – is about focusing on earning enough to cover your real overheads. In this state, all your consumption is necessary. Given that we don't always have control over what we're paid, it makes sense to look first at whether we can help ourselves by needing less, not just by earning more. To see in the short term if we can separate needs (food, water, shelter, fuel) from wants.

JP fervently believes that if you do what you love, remuneration will follow. Blogger Mr Money Mustache certainly found this to be the case, having taken up carpentry after earning enough to retire early.[76] Word got round and he soon found he was being offered more than enough work to **Survive** (although his parents had warned him off carpentry for fear he would end up poor). Naturally, this example of hope might not feel directly useful to someone whose financial means aren't covering their needs: money stress is both debilitating and truly terrifying, as Sara understands from personal experience. Renovating the boat she called home while holding down an underpaid job gave her plenty of practice in separating wants from needs. By first carefully examining and reducing her real needs she realised she had to increase her income in order to complete the restoration project and be able to eat.

---

[74] Meecham, Jesse (2018) *You Need a Budget: the Proven System for Breaking the Paycheck-to-Paycheck Cycle, Getting Out of Debt, and Living the Life You Want,* HarperCollins.

[75] James, Oliver (2008), *The Selfish Capitalist: Origins of Affluenza,* Vermilion.

[76] He's an online thrifty lifestyle expert - check him out he can teach you how better than we can.

TWEAKS FOR YOU

→ What are your real needs and what is their cost? List and calculate the monthly and annual costs for all your needs.[77] Remember: budgets fail because people miss out costs and aren't honest about needs.

→ Do you earn enough to cover your needs? If so, great! Your survival materialism is sorted and you can now proceed to T is for **Thrive**. If not, ask yourself: can you manage on less[78] or earn more?[79]

SHIFTS FOR YOUR TEAM

→ Talk to your team about what they are really trying to achieve with their earnings. Consider including a subscription to a budgeting platform, such as YNAB, in your employee reward package or just raise awareness.

→ There is a lot of talk about the 'sharing economy'.[80] Get yourself and colleagues involved in the real sharing economy by establishing a swap shop where people can bring and take items they need.

JUMPS FOR YOUR ORGANISATION

→ Go beyond paying a Living Wage by setting a minimum salary at a level where everyone can afford to live.

→ Apply the same budget questions to the organisation. What do you spend money on that you don't need to? Where can you reduce impact by sourcing second-hand? How can you increase income?

---

[77] Use a tool such as YNAB to better understand how to budget and keep motivated.

[78] By sharing more, choosing second-hand or delaying needs.

[79] By selling things you no longer need, renting out a room or moving to a better-paid role.

[80] This is a misnomer as it isn't about sharing but about selling access to underused assets.

LET'S ALL LIVE
THE GOOD
LIFE.

T

IS FOR THRIVE

It's one thing to have what it takes to survive economically and another to know what you want more of when you get there. We're not just talking about money and power or the aching **More, More, More!** of selfish consumerism. Or, indeed, any of the limited definitions of success that send countries chasing GDP growth, organisations aggressively pursuing turnover and individuals obsessing over net worth. Rather we mean a broader definition of success, remembering that to truly **Thrive** is to be someone who has 'made room for well-being, wisdom, wonder and giving.'[81] In 'making room', some will want to work more to have more to give away. Perhaps to invest in high-impact charities or new greentech companies. Others might want to work less to have more time to volunteer or practise a craft or go on an adventure. There's no right way to **Thrive**, only wrong ways, given that few of us **Thrive** when we keep increasing our income to meet inflated needs while ignoring our calling and desires. To experience more joy, more beauty, more generosity and true wealth – that's what we call being better off.

What will make you better off in the deepest, broadest sense?
What stops you pursuing true wealth and living the good life?
Once you have the means to meet your needs, ask yourself:
What does that mean to you?
What do you really want?
How will you share the joy?

---

[81] Huffington, Arianna (2015) *Thrive: The Third Metric to Redefining Success and Creating a Happier Life*, WH Allen.

'THE RESTORATION OF WEALTH IN THE MIDST OF AN AFFLUENCE IN WHICH WE ARE STARVING OF THE SPIRIT.' JOHN LANE[82]

It can be hard to **Thrive** as an individual or an organisation in a system that requires constant competition and growth to feel relevant. Economist Kate Raworth has identified the paradox resulting from this: 'Today we have economies that need to grow, whether or not they make us thrive: what we need are economies that make us thrive, whether or not they grow.'[83] Oliver James concurs, noting that, since the 1970s, economic strategy has 'rolled out changes which were designed to pursue GDP growth and make the rich richer. At the same time conditions became worse and hours of work increased.'[84]

In London alone, almost 50 per cent of employment is in small and medium-sized enterprises (SMEs) which account for more than 99 per cent of businesses[85] – a statistic so high you might think we've got it wrong. (We haven't. We double checked!) In our work at Ugli, Bootstrap, Brand Amplifier and WorkWild, we have supported entrepreneurs and employees of SMEs to enable them to **Thrive** – helping them access the space, training and networks that have brought them success in the broadest and truest sense of the word. By supercharging our approach with a focus on thriving, we've been able to ask even young businesses to consider the social impact of their activities by looking to see who in the community they can help.

---

[82] Lane, John (2000) *Timeless Simplicity,* Green Books.

[83] Raworth, Kate (2018) *Doughnut Economics,* Random House Business.

[84] James, Oliver (2008) *The Selfish Capitalist: Origins of Affluenza,* Vermilion.

[85] Department for Business, Energy and Industrial Strategy (2008) *Business Population Estimates for the UK and Regions.*

TWEAKS FOR YOU

→ What security and flexibility do you and those you love or those who rely on you need in the future? Do you have a costed plan of how to keep them safe? If not, make one now, factoring the cost of this into your plan to **Thrive**.

→ Establish what resonates with you and prioritise managing your life and work in such a way as to be able to fund and afford time to do more of the things that enrich your soul and make you and those you love truly better off.

SHIFTS FOR YOUR TEAM

→ Work with your team to explore ways of supporting each other to **Thrive**. List ways to make space and time for this that don't distract from the day job you're in together.

→ Can your team come up with entrepreneurial ideas that support your clients, service users and/or customers to **Thrive**? If you find a strong idea, make a business and impact case for it. If it's got potential, find a way to make it happen.

JUMPS FOR YOUR ORGANISATION

→ Can you fully embrace a commitment to everyone relating to your organisation thriving? What would that look like and how would you measure success? Do you need to change the metrics you use to track your performance?

→ If you're not already a social enterprise, look seriously at becoming one or rebooting your business to make a positive social and/or environmental impact. At the very least, start working towards B Corp certification and go from there.

UNLEASH
YOUR BRAVE
SOUL.

U IS FOR UNDAUNTED

Have the bravery to go your own way. The way that calls to your deepest, most essential self. In a work sense, this means to find your vocation, an enjoyable way to earn a living. It might have been screaming at you (but heeding the call might have seemed too risky) or it might take some unearthing. It might be that you need to hold your nerve and do nothing for as long as you possibly can. Often we are too busy (or too fearful) to step back and find out what we would really like to do. Stop trying and eventually it will call you. That's why it's known as 'a calling'.

To just let things happen can be very daunting, especially if you've been very career focused and are used to being in control and making things happen. Remember that bravery cannot exist without truth. The first step is to admit honestly that you need to do something that fits you and really resonates. Or perhaps you could find a group of people who share your values. Throw yourself in. After all, 'enthusiasm is a form of social courage'.[86]

Feeling out of place is a clue, a whisper, a nudge.
Step out from behind the things that are blocking your view.
What is your gift and how do you acknowledge and honour it?
Have courage to let things float to the surface.
Don't climb ladders.
Grow trees.

---

[86] Rubin, Gretchen (2011) *The Happiness Project,* HarperCollins.

'WITHOUT COURAGE WE CANNOT PRACTISE ANY OTHER VIRTUE WITH CONSISTENCY. WE CAN'T BE KIND, TRUE, MERCIFUL, GENEROUS OR HONEST.' MAYA ANGELOU[87]

A call to be **Undaunted**, to be 'brave and true' like our concept of the **Gentle Warrior**, has existed across human history in many if not all cultures. Models of gentle warriorship, such as the Samurai or the Knights of the Round Table, continue to have resonance today. The need for strong moral codes and to help others are an important part of these traditional warriorship concepts. According to Chögyam Trungpa, who writes about warriorship, 'the tradition of human bravery [is], a tradition of fearlessness with helping others.'[88] The Tibetan word for warrior simply means 'one who is brave'. That doesn't mean you won't feel fear. At times it is quite right and normal, indeed appropriate, to be scared. Remember that nervousness and excitement are very similar physiologically and as Nelson Mandela said: 'I learned that courage was not the absence of fear, but the triumph over it.'[89]

When JP was 11, she very nearly died in a bicycle accident that left her with a handlebar through her side, multiple facial injuries and her family and friends praying for her recovery. This taught her two big life lessons. Having dug up the road with her face, she learned to value people for who they are and not how they look. She also developed an insatiable appetite for living in the moment and taking risk, giving herself permission to pursue what she loved. Maybe acts of bravery and risk-taking are easier if you've had a near-death experience. But can you be truly brave if you have never stared death in the face? Of course! JP thinks it's all about gaining perspective: extreme challenges or daunting experiences force you to step out of normality. When normal life resumes, you have gained a fresh perspective and can perhaps use those experiences to become less risk averse.

---

[87] Angelou, Maya (2011) interview, *O, The Oprah Magazine.*

[88] Trungpa, Chögyam (1988) *Shambhala: Sacred Path of the Warrior*, Random House USA Inc.

[89] Nelson Mandela in a speech to the House of Congress, 1989

TWEAKS FOR YOU

→ Scrapbook, doodle and daydream to conjure up what has resonated for you in your work. Find the themes, places and people that made you feel you were on the right track. The things that made you feel whole and alive are the clues to your vocation.

→ Now list your top three fears and insecurities.[90] Look at them and ask yourself what you would do if these weren't in the way.

SHIFTS FOR YOUR TEAM

→ Start congratulating yourself and each other on your courage at the end of the day. Make it a habit. Celebrate the times when someone spoke up, did the hard thing, channelled their **Gentle Warrior**.

→ Audit the team's skills and passions, and not just the obviously work-related ones. Seek out where there is synergy with the organisation's needs. Is there a chance to develop vocations?

JUMPS FOR YOUR ORGANISATION

→ Craft vocations and seek people who want to grow with you. Reject the concept of the career and its limited definition of success.

→ Adopt bravery as one of your core values. Go on, we dare you!

---

[90] Explore what's behind these – use L is for **Look in the Shadows** to work out what's holding you back/causing the reaction.

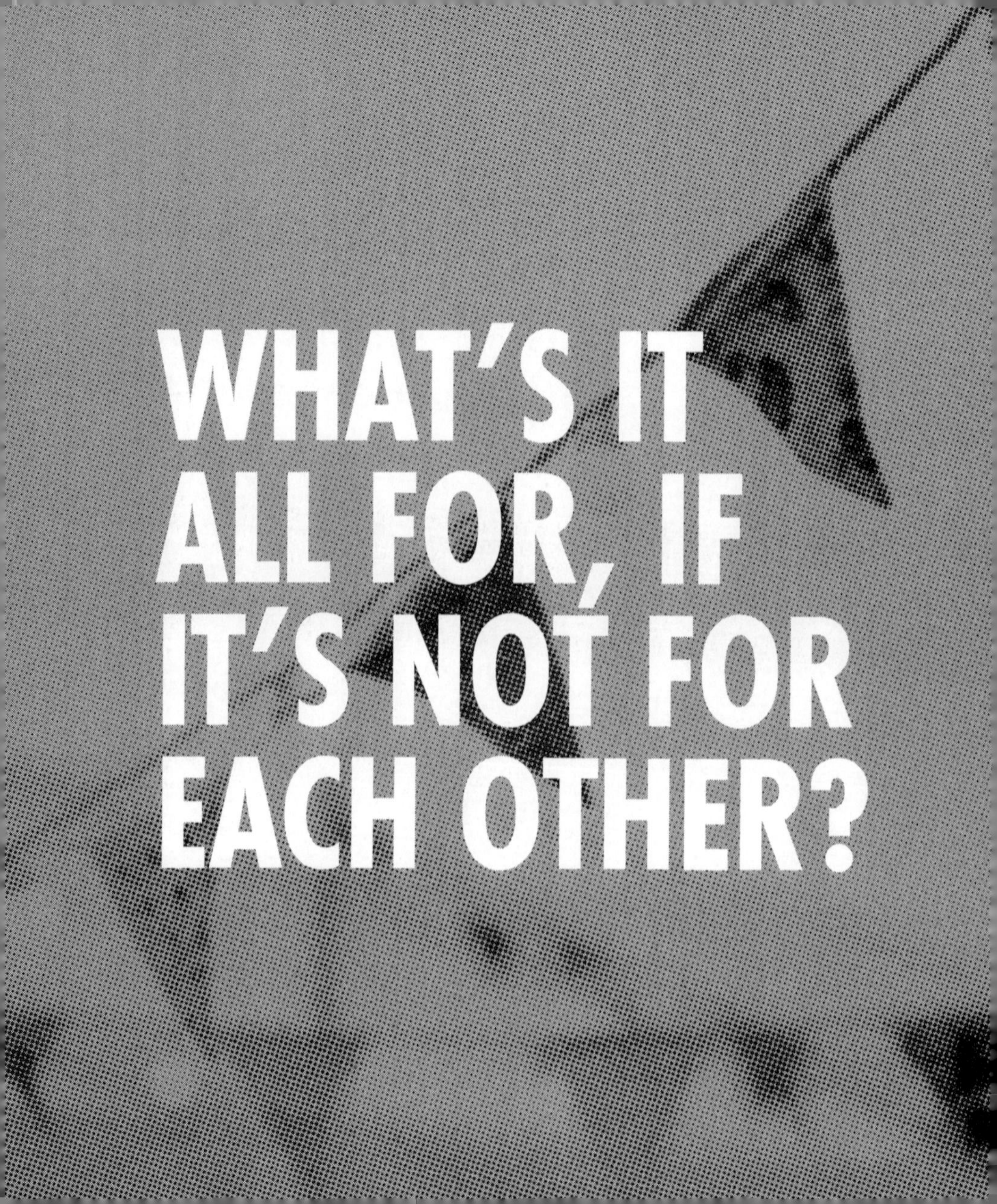
WHAT'S IT ALL FOR, IF IT'S NOT FOR EACH OTHER?

V

IS FOR VILLAGE PEOPLE

Humans like to put down roots wherever they are, be it on a chair in a meeting room, in a home town or a campsite. Given time, these roots help us to bond with and belong to a place. Many of us, however, lack deep roots and the majority of us now live in cities and are more at risk of being caught in a wasteland of emotional, spiritual and physical isolation. But aren't we all still village folk at heart?

When we work, just as when we live, we form 'villages' from the people with whom we work, whether we are in call centres, fields, offices, factories, workshops, engine rooms, dance studios, schools or labs. And what is the workplace if not a village hall? Any organisation needs to design itself in the context of the greater whole – the families it provides for, the societies it serves and is composed of – the **Village People**. What happens when you open the doors to your hall and invite people in? Really invite them in. With the open arms of collective success through profit sharing, employee ownership and coming together in support of each other. Community people. Unity through business.

Small can be powerful. Small but not small-minded.
So go small, people: go village.
Go social enterprise, start-ups and SMEs.
Create belonging, make real jobs and real wealth.
Eradicate the feeling of being lost with togetherness.

'MEDIEVAL CITIES WERE DELIBERATELY FOUNDED ON WHAT WOULD TODAY BE CONSIDERED DANGEROUSLY RADICAL PRINCIPLES. THEY WERE SET UP IN ORDER TO ESCAPE THE RULE OF THE NOBLES AND TO CREATE AN IDEAL WORKING AND CREATIVE COMMUNITY IN WHICH FAIRNESS, EQUALITY AND HELPING EACH OTHER WERE THE DOMINANT ETHICAL PRINCIPLES. WORK WAS ORGANISED AROUND THE GUILDS SYSTEM. THE CITIES HAD A NATURAL LIMIT ON GROWTH BECAUSE THEY WERE WALLED.' TOM HODGKINSON[91]

Whether we live in a literal village or a town or city, we can experience the 'village' feeling of close-knit community. We are social animals that need one another emotionally, physically, practically and even at the level of brain chemistry. The place where we come together is the village, lovely people – born of the celebratory, kitsch, joyful and sometimes dirty need to dance, bond and throw ourselves around; strengthened by humour, camaraderie and sharing. In close-knit communities, we depend on each other and, in doing so, become fluent in each other's flaws and ugly bits while loving each other anyway.

We look increasingly to our places of work for this sense of community. If we find this feeling of belonging, our work can become a huge part of our identity. In the past, many skilled people worked for themselves and came together with local traders in guilds. These days, co-working and community-focused creative and social workspaces enable sole traders and micro-businesses to work alongside, and share with, each other. In all these cases, there is incredible power in working together.

---

[91] Hodgkinson, Tom (2006) *How to be Free*, Penguin.

TWEAKS FOR YOU

→ Imagine you and your colleagues are sitting around a campfire. Sketch out who are your elders and peers and who you'd like to sit next to. Whose wisdom and insights do you want to share and be guided by?

→ Then write a set of questions to ask your elders and peers and invite them for a coffee or lunch, or set up a call. If you can't fit it in, see D is for **Do or Do Not**.

SHIFTS FOR YOUR TEAM

→ Look for the people who are the glue in your team and community. Remember that followers are needed, not just leaders. Reward the people who unite teams and follow great ideas.

→ Create belonging by putting the tea in team! Ensure everyone (or almost everyone) stops for tea and coffee at the same time every day. If possible, also all cook and eat lunch together.

JUMPS FOR YOUR ORGANISATION

→ Focus on growth in the truest sense (growth in skills, impact and community, not just in size or turnover). Procure from small businesses, employee-owned and social enterprises when you can. Consider if you can move towards an Employee Ownership Trust and/or share profit with your people.

→ Think small. Be like Gore (of Goretex) and divide up teams when they reach 150 people.

THE ART
OF SELF-
SUFFICIENCY.

W

IS FOR WHITTLE AND WEAVE

We humans are a crafty bunch and our desire to make things connects to the pleasure of a job well done and our need to **Survive** by providing for ourselves. Historically people as young as eight would knit on the move and in snatches of time between other tasks to 'augment otherwise slender incomes and as a means to an end'.[92] Environmentalist and writer Carol Donaldson writes about 'the satisfaction to be found in self-reliance, that feeling of being a capable woman able to take on a problem and solve it'. This sense of power and autonomy is eroding as we become less self-sufficient. Mourning the loss of skills 'that keep us free men and women', she questions why we work long hours to pay for the things we could do ourselves, in a world where 'the equation between our labour and our lives has got dark and misty.'[93]

There is joy to be had stripping away material to reveal something (whittle = to take things back to reveal usefulness/purpose) or bringing together threads to construct a whole (weave = to meld together and make stronger). To **Whittle and Weave** is a call to arms (or, more accurately, hands) to create what is needed to first **Survive** then **Thrive**.

Hone your craft through sweat and graft.
Strip off the rough edges to reveal beauty and useful purpose.
Every thread is an idea interlocked into the larger fabric.
The bigger picture, our common story.

---

[92] Compton, Rae (1983) *The Complete Book of Traditional Knitting*, The Anchor Press.

[93] Donaldson, Carol (2017) *On the Marshes*, Little Toller Books.

'THE EFFORT TO BRING SOMETHING NEW AND MEANINGFUL INTO THE WORLD – WHETHER IN THE ARTS, THE KITCHEN OR THE MARKETPLACE – IS EXACTLY WHAT GENERATES THE SENSE OF MEANING AND FULFILMENT FOR WHICH SO MANY OF US YEARN SO DEEPLY.' PETER KORN

In today's corporate workplace, 'creative thought and decision making are centralised into the hands of small cohorts of experts [and] work has been stripped of its potential to provide meaning and fulfillment.'[94] It is little wonder then, that so many are drawn back to the world of craft and the hope for the sense of self-respect that comes from making 'a spoon in the morning' and 'selling it in the afternoon' and the fulfilment that comes from being able to 'go out there with just an axe and a knife, and make a living.'[95]

Meet JP as a child, either outside on the Welsh hills or at home in her bedroom, busy making new worlds out of paper pulp egg boxes and sticky tape. One Christmas she was even given rolls of tape because of her reputation for being more interested in making something out of the packaging than the gift itself. Crowned 'Sellotape Queen'[96] by her family as a child, the desire to keep making worlds and models led to making models of sets at the Royal Opera House and London Coliseum. JP had already discovered her wildness in her true creative self. In time, this creative wildness led JP to her vocation, creative entrepreneurship. Here she continues to whittle, honing the creative businesses she develops and works with through mentoring and team development – whittling spoons and crafting on the side all the while.

---

[94] Korn, Peter (2014) *Why We Make Things and Why it Matters,* David R. Godine Publisher Inc.

[95] Barn the Spoon (2017) *Spōn: a Guide to Spoon Carving and the New Wood Culture,* Virgin Books.

[96] The Sellotape Queen was awarded an MBE by her Queen in 2018 for services to business and entrepreneurship.

TWEAKS FOR YOU

→ What are the maintenance skills you pay others for but secretly long to have yourself? Can you develop these to improve your self-sufficiency and create joy?

→ A side hustle can be the way to ensure you have additional income. But beware of making yourself a new job (bringing with it the associated admin) and losing the joy of crafting for its own sake.

SHIFTS FOR YOUR TEAM

→ Keep your 'why' knife sharp: some whittling purists will argue that the pocket knife is the *only* acceptable tool for true whittling. See your role as lead whittler and pare back ideas with the power of Why? Why? Why?

→ How can you get the benefit of craft at work in non-craft roles? What bits of working as a team can you take off machines and devices and turn into crafts and making? How might making it a sensory experience improve thinking and collaboration?

JUMPS FOR YOUR ORGANISATION

→ Look to your collective diversity for the strength that exists within the organisation. In listening to and combining all these strands of thought, you pull together and weave your unique and powerful story.

→ Whittle the story down and use it to structure the company. Tell and retell the story consistently and clearly. Then 'make it so'.

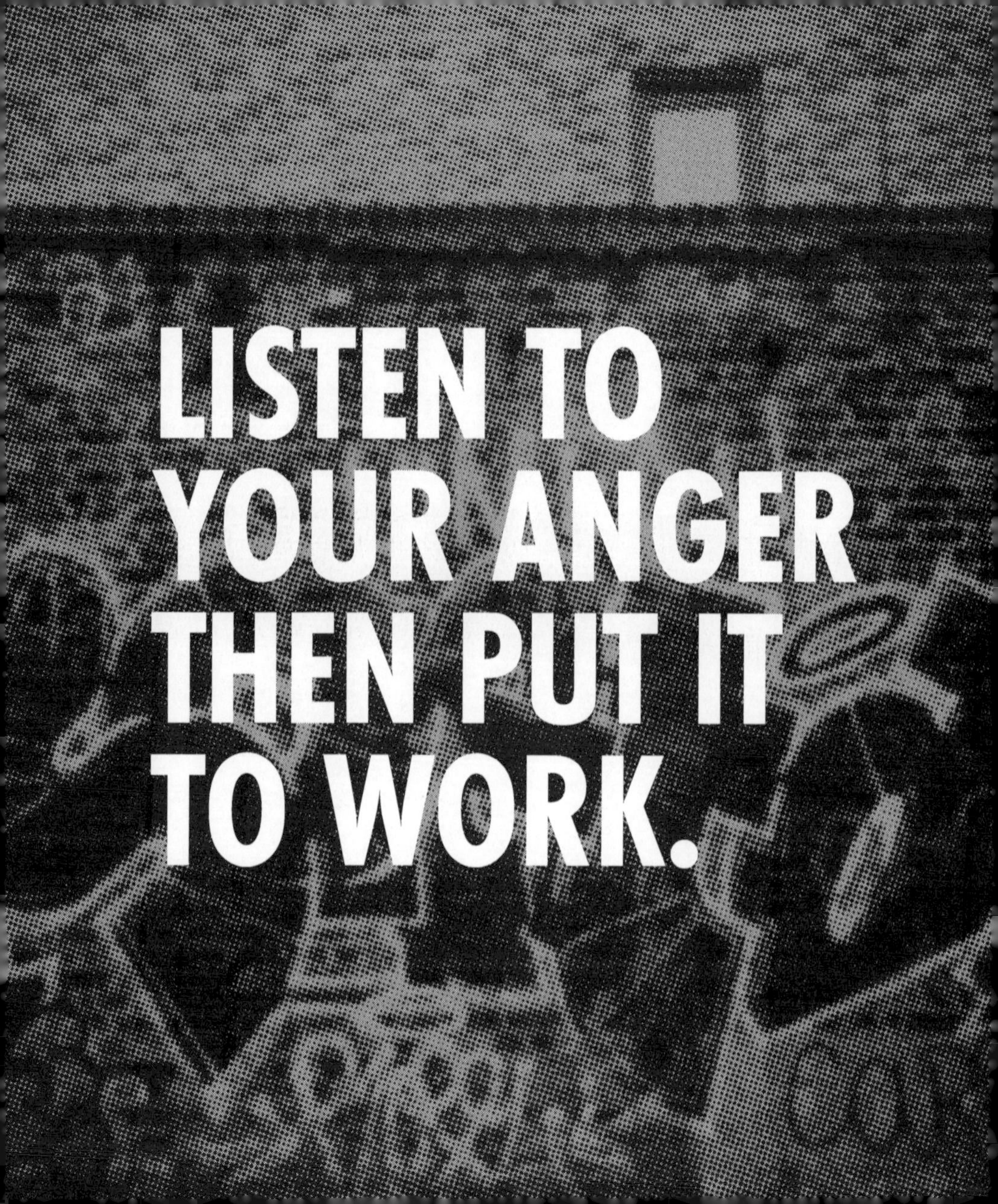
LISTEN TO
YOUR ANGER
THEN PUT IT
TO WORK.

X

IS FOR XXXX IT!

Sometimes just recognising what's wrong in your life or at work is enough to help you reframe things, shift the energy and get back on track. At other times, you may need to work harder to put things right. Researchers at Keele University have proven that swearing can help you tolerate pain for longer and even increase your muscle strength.[97] Meanwhile, many of our best social entrepreneurs channel the anger sparked by injustice to spur them into positive action. Anger + passion = solutions. Find yourself a way to be paid for your solutions (ideally by solving more problems that make you angry) and you've got yourself a social enterprise or a new income stream with a positive impact for your existing organisation. What is your real anger and where does it come from? Can you help change what's wrong with the world? When things aren't going well, start by saying: '**XXXX it!**'

When things hurt and you feel angry, say: 'XXXX it!'
Call it out.
Own it.
Make it yours.
Use your anger to fuel your best work.
Unpick that anger to find the best solution.
A tip for those of you who don't get angry: your passion can be just as good a guide.

---

[97] Stephens, R & Umland, C (2011) 'Swearing as a response to pain - effect of daily swearing frequency', *The Journal of Pain.*

'DON'T GET A BUSINESS DEGREE, GET ANGRY.' ANITA RODDICK[98]

It's crucial to voice what makes you angry and to understand how you can use it to fuel you. Anger is an energy after all. That's why every first interview at WorkWild contains the question: 'What makes you angry?' This question has shaped our lives, businesses and our client work. When we helped set up the Make Shift Foundation, we asked the whole client team to write individual 'angry lists' and stick them on their chests, then to find people who shared their anger and talk about it. We next prompted them to pull out their list of passions (they had penned and pocketed these earlier), compare notes and use their passions to devise solutions to the problems that made them angry. Their creativity in doing this helped us define the activities of their new charity with them.

---

[98] Roddick, Anita (2006) 'Don't get a business degree, get angry,' *Financial Times,* 14 November.

TWEAKS FOR YOU

→ List everything that has made you angry today, this week, this month, this year. Identify the central themes and patterns in your 'angry list' and ask yourself why they make you angry and what you can do about them.

→ Make yourself a 'Stop! Start! Carry on!' list that helps you determine what to tackle first from your angry list. Set a date with a good friend to talk things over and work out the one killer action you can take to address what makes you angry. Take it. Start to feel good about where your anger can take you when you channel it well. Look for more anger to tame.

SHIFTS FOR YOUR TEAM

→ Try out the 'anger and passions' approach described above in a workshop with your team and a group of internal and external clients and colleagues. Use the workshop to establish a common vision on the topics and groups you care about.

→ Maintain an open dialogue with your team about anger and passions, helping individual team members to channel their strongest emotions to feed ideas, strengthen their relationships and make an impact on your organisation.

JUMPS FOR YOUR ORGANISATION

→ Embrace anger gently and make it useful at work by using it to identify problems to unlock and address together.

→ Set up and fund (with food and drink) '**XXXX it!** Salons'. These could be bi-monthly events where people can talk about what's making them angry and work together to find positive solutions. Use them to feed into your organisation's existing work to increase innovation, support the greater autonomy of teams and establish a healthy culture around managing emotions and feelings at work.

THIS ISN'T
A DRESS
REHEARSAL
AND YOU'RE
THE DIRECTOR.

Y

IS FOR YOUR TIME

Tick tock, tick tock. One eye on the clock? Although time at work often seems like a series of deadlines and to-do lists, life (including work) really is no more than a series of nows, with only you – your breath, your will, your decisions and your actions – linking those nows together to create your life. It's a production in which you are at once the star, stage hand and director, so don't script a show that saves all the good stuff for **When I Retire**. Be careful not to wish your life away by counting the number of sleeps until your next holiday, the number of years until retirement or the number of weeks until you can hand in your notice without losing your bonus. Instead, **Own Your Breath**. The time you have is your most precious commodity, so make it mean something. Think about what thrills and connects you and what you really, really want to enable you to live your most joyful, wild and juicy life.

Graphic designer Stefan Sagmeister has done just that: he takes a year-long sabbatical every seven years, having pragmatically batched up his retirement into chunks brought forward to enjoy earlier in life. This feeds not just his soul but his creative practice (which feeds his commercial success). Who couldn't get wild about an approach like that?

Don't wish your (work) life away.
Own your time and own your breath.
Be your own Time Lord and ring-fence your time.
While you still have time.

'TIME IS OUR MOST PRECIOUS POSSESSION. TO GIVE SOMEBODY YOUR TIME IS TO GIVE HIM OR HER PART OF THAT PRECIOUS THING. YOU CAN ONLY OFFER SUCH A GIFT BY SIMPLIFYING YOUR LIFE SO YOU HAVE TIME FOR YOURSELF AND MORE, AGAIN, TO GIVE AWAY.' DIANA BERESFORD-KROEGER[99]

While employed at Arup, Sara proposed moving to a four-day week. She had jam to make, knitting to do and, most importantly, she wanted to sleep in a bed again – not under a desk. When her manager not only accepted the request but offered to pay her at the same rate,[100] Sara quickly became the go-to person for other colleagues wanting to do the same. (Some of them stayed on at Arup precisely because of this flexibility, which gave them the freedom to grow as consultants while having their own rock band.) Even with a four-day week, work and life admin often spill over and there still doesn't seem to be enough time for the 'good life'. We are all trying to do too much.

Going back to fundamentals: instead of all of us trying to do everything, why not try the 50:50 approach? This could be half a day on and half a day off. Or working half a week. Or six months on, six months off. In JP's case, 50:50 is half in Suffolk, half in London. Miracle Mornings, an approach developed by Hal Elrod,[101] has enabled JP to edge towards a manageable 50:50 life. By waking early, she can harness the quiet hours from 4am and channel them into a series of morning rituals that help her make the best of her time before the rest of the family is awake.

---

[99] Beresford-Kroeger, Diana (reprint 2015) *The Sweetness of a Simple Life,* Vintage Books Canada.

[100] Being super ethical (and at that time really undervaluing her own time) Sara said no because saying yes would have made her feel like she had to work on the fifth day. She often did anyway. D'oh.

[101] Elrod, Hal (2016) *The Miracle Morning: the 6 Habits that will Transform Your Life Before 8am,* Hodder & Stoughton.

TWEAKS FOR YOU

→ Use time in a way that fits your rhythm, be that Miracle Mornings, a work-from-home day, mini break, extended holiday or sabbatical.

→ Would you like to change your working hours – trading income for flexibility? If you have a partner, can you evolve your economy together to afford a four-day week or even a 50:50 life?

SHIFTS FOR YOUR TEAM

→ Ask your team what flexibility it needs to give its best at home as well as work. Work with clients to make this achievable on a long-term basis.

→ Use out-of-office and voicemail messages in a more human way to be clear about working hours and expectations, for example: 'I work a four-day week,' or 'As a parent, I work unusual hours.'

JUMPS FOR YOUR ORGANISATION

→ Consider introducing a four-day week. What organisational changes do you need to make? Might a nine-day fortnight be a good first step?

→ Offer parents (perhaps everyone) the option to go 50:50 either in time or location if your business can get by without everyone being in the same place all the time.

GO TO SLEEP,
CLOSE YOUR
EYES.

Z

IS FOR ZZZZZ

Sleep is an essential part of our natural rhythm – it reduces stress, increases creativity and contributes to a longer, fuller life – yet almost a fifth of people employed in industrialised countries work shifts. This pitches them against their in-built body clock, with negative impacts on sleep patterns and health.[102] People with insomnia are shown in one Dutch report to be 56 per cent more likely to have impaired work performance[103] but the effects of loss of sleep don't end there: sleeplessness affects behaviour, with workplace harassment, bullying and unwanted sexual attention shown, across a range of studies, to be associated with poor sleep. And, of course, sleep doesn't just set you up for the next working day. A good night of seven to nine hours' sleep heals you, helping you to learn, improving problem solving and warding off diseases such as cancer and Alzheimer's. Sleep does more than simply aid good decision making and help you be at your calmest, most invigorated best in the workplace: it helps you to live longer.[104]

Take care to recharge your own battery the way you charge your phone.
Don't join the moody people (half of whom are moody from lack of sleep).
Take sleep seriously. Put yourself to bed like you would a child.
Wake up a lovelier version of yourself (and a much easier one to work with).

---

[102] Garbarino, S and Magnavita, N (2017) 'Sleep, health and wellness at work', *International Journal of Environmental Research and Public Health.*

[103] Hoogendijk, WJ and Van Mill, JG (2013) 'Sleep disturbances and reduced work functioning in depressive or anxiety disorders', *Sleep Medicine.*

[104] Walker, Matthew (2018) *Why We Sleep*, Penguin

'WE HAVE STIGMATISED SLEEP WITH THE LABEL OF LAZINESS.' MATTHEW WALKER

We need sleep and yet there is a sleep-loss epidemic throughout industrialised nations.[105] This isn't just hearsay or life experience (although we value both) but an evolving science. Matthew Walker, the guru of sleep science, identifies a great example of a company taking sleep seriously. Aetna, an insurance company with 50,000 employees, awards bonuses based on sleep-tracker data to incentivise staff to get a good night's rest every night. CEO Mark Bertolini explains: 'Being present in the workplace and making better decisions has a lot to do with our business fundamentals ... You can't be prepared if you're half asleep,' before going on to talk about the return on sleep investment (now that's a metric we'd love boards to adopt!) and advocating the need for companies to move away from the 16- to 18-hour workday that burns out staff 'in a model of disposability and declining productivity, littered with sick days, all the while triggering low morale and high turnover rates.'[106]

The science and the economics are clear. In addition to helping with performance, retention and morale, sleep actually unlocks new ideas. Paul McCartney famously came up with the melody for *Yesterday* in a dream[107] and Sara has experienced new Japanese words coming to her in dreams – words she didn't know she knew yet. All in all, 'I'll sleep when I'm dead' is surely the most ill-advised motto ever.

---

[105] Cookson, C, Jack, A and Dodd, D (2017) 'The silent epidemic of sleep loss', *Financial Times,* 6 October.

[106] Walker, Matthew (2018) *Why We Sleep,* Penguin.

[107] McNulty, Bernadette (2016) 'The life of a song: *Yesterday*', *Financial Times,* 6 November.

TWEAKS FOR YOU

→ Go to sleep. Really make a deal with yourself to get the right amount of quality sleep. If you're into your tech, by all means track your sleep if that helps motivate you. Use **Airplane Mode** in the bedroom at all times. If, like us, you struggle to sleep at the time of the full moon, work with that – harness the power and go into that phase rested.

→ Keep track of your work hours so they don't spill into your sleep hours. Flag it if they do: although it's sometimes OK to push, you can't push for too long (see D is for **Do or Do Not** if you need to cut down on your workload).

SHIFTS FOR YOUR TEAM

→ Recognise when staff are at their most productive and allow flexitime to enable owls and larks to work at their best times. Give special care to new parents and grieving members of the team.

→ You'll still need to make sure you can get work done well, so make sure you have space and time to collaborate and produce.

JUMPS FOR YOUR ORGANISATION

→ Adapt your workspace to provide space to sleep/nap/rest at work. In the summer this could be a place to doze outside; in the winter you might need to think more carefully about this. Hospitals and security teams often have a rest or on-call room – should your organisation have one too?

→ Introduce the US model of duvet days, where 'no questions asked' rest days can be taken a number of times a year. Sometimes sleep is more important than anything.

04

GO FOR IT!

Of course, it's no good just reading about it. It's time to go for it!

Unless, of course, you've already started. Perhaps you are one of those people who jumps in and out of a book, trying and testing ideas and tools as they go. In that case, we hope you've found some tools you like in the A-Z and have already started building a good attitude and making changes to the way you work at the individual, team or organisational level. If that is you, perhaps now you are wondering how to keep up the momentum or get more systematic.

Or maybe you've read though this book in order but are still unsure of where to begin or how to get permission to start. That's the point of this section: it is here to give you permission and support.

If you need a method, here it is: just two simple steps to get you going.

1. Address the biggest problem(s) (focus on the change you most need).
2. Effect sustainable change (make it last and make it matter).

After all, it's your life and you can, and do, make the choices. So effect the change you want to see. Now's the time to really go for it and fix what isn't working for you.

Address the biggest problem(s)

Use the table on the following pages to identify the best Working Wild attitudes and tools to get you started, working on the biggest problems you currently face. Think about something specific you are struggling with at work at the moment (if you aren't sure or there are too many problems, take a look back at your self-diagnosis at the beginning of the book). This can be something you struggle with as an individual or it could be something you are in charge of sorting out for your team.

Working out the top problem(s) to address will tell you where to start, and the table will help you find and record what tools and attitudes you need to effect the change. If you need support (and buy-in[108]) to make this all happen, work out what you need and how to get it. Then go for it!

[108] Yikes! Having got this far without any work jargon, we just couldn't help it with this one!

Top problem(s)	How Working Wild can help
1	*Top attitude(s) to cultivate* *Top three tools to use from the A–Z* *1* *2* *3*
2	*Top attitude(s) to cultivate* *Top three tools to use from the A–Z* *1* *2* *3*
3	*Top attitude(s) to cultivate* *Top three tools to use from the A–Z* *1* *2* *3*

How to go for it
By myself I can… *With support of my friend/partner I could…* *If I worked with my team or manager we could…*
By myself I can… *With support of my friend/partner I could…* *If I worked with my team or manager we could…*
By myself I can… *With support of my friend/partner I could…* *If I worked with my team or manager we could…*

Effect sustainable change

We've talked a lot about how the broken world of work is affecting us, our economy and the planet. Here is where you can plan how Working Wild will create sustainable change for you, your organisation and the wider community.

Working Wild is for everyone – whatever your income, responsibilities, working and financial situation – and also for the planet. For everyone to be better off in the ways that matter – ways that are genuinely sustainable – you need tools and attitudes that help you or your team make a positive impact across the triple bottom line of sustainability: environment, economy and society.

The table opposite shows an example selection of tools and attitudes for effecting sustainable change at a personal, team and organisational level. We've laid these out in a way to help you identify the little things you can start right now, those that may require permission or help from others to build strong foundations as well as some seriously wild tools and attitudes that require everyone to get radical.

A suggestion from us			
	Environment	**Economy**	**Society**
Little things you can start right now	Out There	Survive	Do or Do Not
Build strong foundations	Rebel Rebel	Thrive	Your Time – four-day week
Get radical	Naughty and Naked	In Service	Your Time – 50:50

If you think these will work for you or your organisation, go for it! Soon you will be able to make a shift in your relationship with work. If you think that these won't quite work for you or your team, what do you think will?

Use the blank tables below to record your thinking now and make your own game plan. You can mix tools and attitudes just as we have. Rope in a friend or colleague to help you do the exercise if you'd really like to get support to make this work. Remember you can do this for yourself and for your organisation, hence the two blank tables with space for you to put in the right tools and attitudes for each.

For yourself			
	Environment	**Economy**	**Society**
Little things you can start right now			
Build strong foundations			
Get radical			

For your team or organisation			
	Environment	**Economy**	**Society**
Little things you can start right now			
Build strong foundations			
Get radical			

You might also like to set a date with yourself to come back, check and celebrate progress.

Wildly ever after

We committed ourselves to Working Wild while writing this book. When we got stuck during the creative process, we used the tools to shift us into a better way of working.

We started out with a simple mission and a common cause. First, to help you find a better way of working that works for you. But also to enlist you as **Gentle Warriors** in the fight to fix a **Broken Work** system; one that has left us facing not one but five crises – climate change, the speed of change, threats to biodiversity and food security, disconnection and the lack of a common story. While we can't claim that Working Wild fixes all the crises by itself, we are sure that changing the way we work will help us create positive solutions to address them.

By rewilding first yourself and then your organisation, and rebalancing how you spend your time and money, you can begin to reduce consumption and increase your positive contribution to society and the economy. At the very least, by adopting a Working Wild approach (for yourself, your team and your organisation) that collectively unpicks and rebuilds the way you work, you can challenge the status quo and adopt better ways of living and working.

We hope this book has brought you a sense of authority and the approval to be yourself. It's OK to embrace your wildness and bring it to work. So love what you do – 50 years is a long time to spend doing something you don't like, pretending to be someone you are not and propping up a system that makes us all worse off.

If ever you should feel in doubt of your direction, step back, breathe deeply and ask yourself a simple question. What is the best way to approach my work right now: a way that allows me to remember I am human and to reconnect with work based on a gentler use of resources and time? Just that question alone has the power to help you begin to turn your back on the world of **Broken Work** and unfurl into the world of **Working Wild**.

Once you've got it, you can step into your power and work and lead in a different way. Then you can take these attitudes and tools for Working Wild deeper and also wider, extending them beyond yourself to your friendships, family and your wider community. It's irresistible!

About Sara

Sara Turnbull is a swimmer, chartered environmentalist, social entrepreneur and an award winning leader in sustainability and social value. Sara leads and shapes social enterprises, charities and other organisations committed to creating a more sustainable world. She has woven together work in architecture and engineering, affordable workspace, venues and events, and community development. As a passionate speaker, consultant and non-executive she is committed to addressing climate change and the wealth gap by delivering work that makes places and organisations better for everyone. She speaks Japanese and is a keen sailor who dreams of more life afloat, being a builder and growing a forest. She likes swimming anywhere (ideally outdoors and naked), sailing anything (preferably wooden), riding waves (and bikes) and dancing (barefoot).

About JP

Jeannette Pearce's 25 years' experience spans from nationally acclaimed theatre designer to founder of multiple award winning businesses in the marketing communications, experiential, hotels, business campus, co-working and charitable sectors. She was awarded an MBE in November 2018 for her services to business and entrepreneurship. She is a writer, speaker, and consultant, advising businesses and business owners on 'better ways' to operate 21st century organisations that desire to be more social, sustainable, profitable, responsible and resilient. She is married to Nick, her partner in life and also in business and is mum to two teenage sons, Finn and Basti. As a family their latest wild adventure together finds them sympathetically renovating and re-wilding a cottage and smallholding in the foothills of a 10th century castle in Suffolk.

Thanks

We'd like to thank our families, friends and the WorkWild and JPC teams who have supported and inspired us for the year that we were writing. In particular we'd like to thank those who dedicated so much time to help us shape this book. To Tom, Nick, Aifric, Jan and Mel who helped us shape our thoughts and read through early drafts. To the production team: Tracey and Maria for their sharp knives and eagle eyes on copyediting and proofreading, Nic for the design and Josh and Jordan for publishing. Special credit to Nick, Andy, Basti and Finn for giving us the space and time to enable us to write.

Better Off Club

Better Off Working Wild is the first in a series of digests that pulls together rich thinking, evidence and the very best of old-school and contemporary approaches to identify practical solutions and actions to create a better more sustainable way to live. The Better Off Club is for everyone on a mission to campaign and co-create a world in which we can all be truly Better Off. Not in the traditional narrow monetary sense of the word, but in richness of soul, community, family, environment and togetherness. You can find out more, join us and contribute time and ideas at www.thebetteroffclub.com

Printed in Poland
by Amazon Fulfillment
Poland Sp. z o.o., Wrocław

64750325R00092